FATAL DISTRACTIONS

OVERCOMING OBSTACLES THAT MESS UP OUR LIVES

ED YOUNG

Publishers Since 1798

THOMAS NELSON PUBLISHERS®
Nashville

Published in Nashville, Tennessee, by Thomas Nelson, Inc.

Unless otherwise noted Scripture quotations are from THE NEW KING JAMES VERSION. Copyright © 1979, 1980, 1982, Thomas Nelson, Inc., Publishers.

Scripture quotations noted TLB are from *The Living Bible*, copyright © 1971. Used by permission of Tyndale House Publishers, Inc., Wheaton, Illinois 60189. All rights reserved.

Scripture quotations noted NASB are from the NEW AMERICAN STANDARD BIBLE ®, © Copyright The Lockman Foundation 1960, 1962, 1963, 1968, 1971, 1972, 1973, 1975, 1977. Used by permission.

Scripture quotations noted NIV are taken from the HOLY BIBLE, NEW INTERNATIONAL VERSION ®. Copyright © 1973, 1978, 1984 by International Bible Society. Used by permission of Zondervan Bible Publishing House. All rights reserved.

The "NIV" and "New International Version" trademarks are registered in the United States Patent and Trademark Office by International Bible Society. Use of either trademark requires the permission of International Bible Society.

Library of Congress Cataloging-in-Publication Data

Young, Ed, 1961–
    Fatal distractions : overcoming the seven deadly sins / Ed Young.
      p. cm.
    ISBN 0-7852-7666-1 (pbk.)
    1. Sins. 2. Christian Life. I. Title.

BV4625'.Y68 2000   99-059855
241'.3—dc21   CIP

Printed in the United States of America
1 2 3 4 5 6 QPV 05 04 03 02 01 00

CONTENTS

This book is dedicated to two gentlemen who lived life abundantly in Christ here on earth and who now celebrate their residency in heaven with our Savior.

To Virtus Gideon, an outstanding seminary professor who encouraged and motivated me to "go for it" in my studies and ministry. Virtus spoke and lived eloquently wisdom and truth in the classroom of life.

And now, to the memory of my father-in-law, Mendel Lee, who mirrored the majesty of his Maker in all of his endeavors. Mendel's "Christ likeness" continues to be an inspiration in our lives and in the lives of our children.

See you soon!

INTRODUCTION

A Look in the Mirror of Our Own Souls

Get real!"

"To be honest with you . . ."

"Don't skirt the issue."

How many times have we heard these phrases and even used them ourselves?

Yet in most cases, we use these sentences about someone other than ourselves. This book challenges you to get real about *you,* to be really honest with yourself about yourself, and to stop skirting the issues that are serious distractions in your life.

Distractions?

Yes. Distractions that keep you from living up to your full potential. Distractions that keep you from experiencing all of the good things that God has for you. Distractions that keep you mesmerized by mediocrity, guilt, and self-justification. Ultimately these distractions can destroy the soul, and for that reason, they are *deadly* distractions.

Are you willing to put the spotlight on yourself?

Are you willing to face up to some things that have dogged you and you have hoped would go away, but haven't?

Are you willing to own up to some attitudes and behaviors that you prefer to remain undiscovered by others, especially those you love the most, but that you know will be found out eventually?

Are you willing to quit swimming in the shallow water and to move to the deep end?

If you can answer yes, then read on!

If you are looking for a book to use to hit another person over the head psychologically, this book isn't for you. If you are looking for a book that tells you that you can live any way you desire and still "have it all" in this life and in the next, this book isn't for you. And if you are looking for a book that tells you that living a pure life in an impure world is a pipe dream, this book isn't for you.

Let me state it plainly right up front: I believe you can live what the world calls a "good life," and you can live what God calls a "right life." You can be free of the things that are hanging you up. But to be free, you can *and must* own up to the distractions described in this book.

We rarely recognize our own shortcomings or sins. That's the crafty, devious nature of sin. Sin lies about itself. It tells the person who is sinning that he is okay and that everything will be all right in the end. Sin points to the law of averages, saying, "Everybody is doing this," or "I'm not as bad as most people are."

The fact is *we want to be perfect.* We want to be little gods ruling over our own universe. We don't want to admit that we have any problems in our personalities, errors in our attitudes, or failures in our behaviors. To admit sin would shatter the persona we have of ourselves.

The fact is also this: *No one is perfect.* And occasionally we need a reality check on that fact. We need to take a long, hard look in a reality mirror—and not just the reality that the world defines but the reality that God defines. We need to see ourselves for who we really are. When we do that, we are going to see some things we don't like. The good news is that we will also run into a two-part hope that God offers: (1) We don't need to remain the way we are, and (2) we can become much more than we are at present if we will do things God's way.

Paul gave Timothy this advice: "Take heed to yourself and to the doctrine. Continue in them, for in doing this you will save both yourself and those who hear you" (1 Tim. 4:16).

I challenge you today:

- Choose to unravel your complex emotions.

- Choose to get to the core of who you really are as a person.

- Choose to identify what motivates you, how you respond to life, and what holds you back from a deeper relationship with other people and with God.

If you'll choose to confront what is standing between you and God, and between your present self and the self you can become, I guarantee that God will help you with *all* of His power, wisdom, and love. And that's a lot of power!

ACKNOWLEDGMENTS

Thank you to Louanne LeBourgeous for keeping me on track and on schedule during the daily grind.

Thank you to Leslie Nunn for her attention to details and deadlines.

To Stan Durham, thank you for continuous creativity.

To the staff of Fellowship Church, thank you for tweaking ideas and helping me with the editing process.

Many, many thanks to the great people of Fellowship Church who allow me, a fellow struggler, to lead and teach each week.

Thank you to my family . . . Mom and Dad who have encouraged and cheered every endeavor of my life. Elva, my wonderful mother-in-law, who laughs at my stories over bountiful meals. Ben and Elliott, Cliff and Danielle, Smith and Laurie, whose support is invaluable and whose lives provide great illustrations.

And finally, to my loving and devoted wife, Lisa, and our precious children, LeeBeth, E. J., Landra, and Laurie, I say "Thank you" and "I love you." You are truly the greatest treasures God has given to me.

1

FATAL DISTRACTIONS

What Is Lurking Unseen?

Recently I took a trip to the Yucatan Peninsula. It turned out to be a hair-raising adventure. I was with two friends, one of whom lived there. We were fishing in waters that were hundreds of miles away from any civilization. All of a sudden, my friend shouted to us, "Ed, David—freeze! Don't even move your eyeballs!" His voice was intense, and David and I did exactly as we were told.

Within a few moments, I heard a loud buzzing over my head and felt a light breeze in the air, but I didn't flinch an inch to take a look in the direction of the sound. Gradually the sound subsided, and my friend said, "You can relax now. You have just survived a massive swarm of African killer bees that flew a few feet over your heads." Off in the distance we could see the swarm making its way toward an offshore island.

The sight was especially frightening to me because I am highly allergic to bee stings, and we were floating on a reef with only about six inches of water below us, not enough to cover me if I had jumped out of the boat.

Many people, I believe, are like I was that day—relaxed and carefree as I was fishing with friends in a beautiful environment. We aren't aware of the killer sins that are lurking deep in our souls and that are swarming and preparing to burst out on the horizon of our lives. I had no idea that African killer bees would be swarming that far out over the waters of the Caribbean. Most people aren't remotely aware that sin is eating away at them on the inside, doing an insidious amount of damage just below the surface of their conscious awareness. Ignorance about the effects of sin can be devastating, and yes, deadly.

THE WORD NOBODY LIKES TO TALK ABOUT

Sin. It's a word that nobody likes to talk about, few want to admit, and fewer still are willing to confront. It takes a courageous person to own up to sin and to seek to do something about it.

In spite of our denial, or our wishing and hoping it

will go away, sin exists and it persists. It is not a nightmare from which we can awaken. It is not a figment of a philosopher's imagination. Sin is reality.

Neither is sin a vague force nor a dark side that exists somewhere, out there, unseen, and unknown. Sin is definable. In the Bible, God sets before mankind very specific attitudes and behaviors that He regards as sin. The attitudes and behaviors are contrary to His plan and purpose for men and women. The attitudes and behaviors hurt our lives, hurt the lives of others, and ultimately sadden the heart of God.

Sin is not some type of consensus agreement about what is right and wrong. God did not conduct a CNN poll, put together a focus group, or issue a questionnaire to mankind prior to His stating the nature, consequences, and definition of sin. God measures sin solely against His perfect and righteous character.

Two General Categories of Fatal Distractions

Two basic types of sins are identified in the Bible: sins of commission and sins of omission. Sins of commission are sins that we willfully and knowingly commit against God's directives. When we engage in a sin of commission, we know what is right and wrong, and we choose to do wrong.

Sins of omission are things that we could have, would

have, or should have done, but we didn't do them. We knew what was right to do, but we failed to do it. We didn't engage in evil. Rather, we did nothing. And in doing nothing, we allowed evil to go unchecked.

I firmly believe that we sin in the area of omission far more than we sin in the area of commission. Most of us are so busy going about our daily lives that we rarely stop to take stock of ourselves, our families, our communities, or our world at large. We don't do drugs, work as prostitutes, commit murder, run with gangs, embezzle from our companies, rob the local convenience store, set off bombs that kill innocent people, beat a spouse and/or children, or do any other thing that we would call evil behavior. In fact, we rarely think about such things.

Many of us glance over the list of the Ten Commandments, and we quickly conclude, *I'm okay.* We haven't committed murder or adultery. We haven't stolen anything, told lies about our neighbors in a court of law, or coveted a neighbor's possessions, at least to the point of acting on that covetousness. We occasionally break the Sabbath, but we justify that by saying, "Everybody does it." We try to honor our fathers and mothers, at least according to our definition of what it means to honor another person. We give lip service to loving God, and we don't keep carved idols around, at least not the type that people had in Bible times. We don't take the name of the Lord in vain, at least not routinely, although an occasional swear word might slip out of our mouths.

But what about the inner sins that are just as deadly because they are the root of the outward sinful behaviors? What are we doing about our sinful attitudes?

We don't willfully go out and commit an act of pride. But how many of us compare ourselves to someone who is down-and-out and say, "Thank God, I'm not like that person!"?

We don't awaken in the morning and say, "Today, I think I'll commit the sin of envy." But how many of us see something belonging to another person and say, "Wow! I wish that were mine"?

Whether the sin is one of attitude or behavior, the net result is the same. The apostle Paul stated it very plainly: "The wages of sin is death, but the gift of God is eternal life in Christ Jesus our Lord" (Rom. 6:23).

Sin produces death. The process may be slow or fast, it may be obvious or subtle, it may be painful in varying degrees, it may take specific forms of brutality, but the grinding wheel of sin tears down a person's soul until it is dust.

Even if no evil behaviors erupt immediately from an evil heart, the sin in an evil heart can kill a person. God looks upon the heart and judges the issues of the heart. The heart reflects who we *are;* actions reflect merely what we *do.* And who we *are* is always a much more powerful descriptor and predictor of our lives.

What are the deadly sins of the heart?

Pride.

Anger.

Envy.

Slothfulness

Lust.

Gluttony.

Greed.

Seven fatal distractions. Alias seven mortal sins. Alias seven death-causing sins of the heart.

Now, there is no one verse in the Bible that lists these seven deadly sins. Who created this list? It initially came from a group of theologians in the Middle Ages. They studied the Bible in search of attitudes and character traits that were considered to be deadly to a person's relationship with God. They looked for sins that kill a person's spiritual potential, cut off a person's ability to enter into the fullness of God's blessings, and drive a wedge between a person and God. These seven sins rose to the top. They are addressed in a number of places throughout the Bible, and in each case, the sin is one that *God* defines as a death-causing attitude.

None of these sins are unpardonable or an inevitable ruler over our lives. Each of these sinful attitudes can be addressed, confessed, forgiven by God, and overcome by the believer who will rely on God's help.

What we do know about these sins is that each of them exists in every human heart to some degree at some time. Each of them is a part of our interior landscape, solely because we are born as children of Adam and Eve, "fallen" men and women who are born with a sin nature.

What we also know about these sins is that each of them has the potential to do great harm to us personally, and that when we manifest behaviors arising from these sinful attitudes, we in turn will do great emotional harm to others, very often to those we love the most.

If allowed to exist and grow in us, these sins will overtake us, overwhelm us, and eventually destroy us from the inside out. The good news is that God has made a way for us to be freed from sin's ugly and evil influence, and also freed from its eternal and deadly consequences.

DEALING WITH OUR HEART PROBLEM

Repeatedly the children of Israel were on a roller coaster of rebellion against God. Deception crept into their hearts, they turned away from God and stopped heeding the statutes of God, and before long, they were doing the exact opposite of what the Lord had commanded them to do. Their rebellion always ended in disaster, pain, and heartache. But long before it reached that point, God would send a prophet—again and again, generation after generation—to warn the people. The prophet conveyed a message, usually along these lines: "You need to repent. You need to turn from your sin."

A sign of repentance in those days was to pour dust over one's head and to rip one's garment. So, from time to time, the children of Israel ripped their T-shirts and said they were going to change their lives. They'd go through the motions of saying the right words and doing the right things, but before long, they rebelled. They dishonored God once again with their relationships, finances, attitudes, and above all, worship. The cycle was—and still is—a vicious one.

Then God called a prophet by the name of Joel to confront the disobedience of the children of Israel and to get to the root of the problem. Joel went before the nation and essentially said, "Folks, you don't have simply a behavior problem, you have a heart problem. You don't need to tear your shirts anymore or pour dust on your heads. You need to tear your hearts before God in true sorrow for your sins. You need to get to the real issue that is causing you to become separated from God, and that ultimately is causing you great disaster, pain, and heartache."

That is the challenge before us today. We must attempt to remedy not only the surface problems of our lives—the things that are visible, annoying to us, and problematic at times—but also the true invisible problems. The fatal distractions are rooted deep inside us. They are grounded in our attitudes and our core feelings. They grow into behaviors that are external and visible, but the root of the problem is internal and invisible.

The prophet Joel held out a great hope for the children of Israel if they would truly deal with their heart problem. He gave this word of the Lord:

"Now, therefore," says the LORD,
"Turn to Me with all your heart,
With fasting, with weeping, and with mourning."
So rend your heart, and not your garments;
Return to the LORD your God.
For He is gracious and merciful,
Slow to anger, and of great kindness;
And He relents from doing harm.
Who knows if He will turn and relent,
And leave a blessing behind Him? (Joel 2:12–14)

The Lord's response to our addressing the sin in our lives is not a response of judgment and harsh punishment. His response anytime we seek His forgiveness and seek to repent of our sins and follow Him is a response of mercy, kindness, forgiveness—yes, even blessing!

It takes real courage to get to the root of what is wrong in our lives, but the benefit of having that courage is immense!

Are you brave enough to face the seven fatal distractions?

PRIDE

Awakening from the Ultimate Bad Trip

Fellowship Church is located near the Dallas–Fort Worth International Airport, and recently as I was on my drive home from the church, I paused to watch some of the planes take off and land. I was in an introspective mood as I watched thousands and thousands of people take trips to various destinations across the country and around the world. Some, I knew, were flying on business. Others were taking trips for pleasure. A few were traveling to visit sick relatives or attend funerals, and a few were children.

As I watched the planes, the thought struck me, *Every person alive is either now on or has been on a unique trip. It's* not a popular trip to admit you've taken. We take it, though, at some point in our lives. It's the ego trip.

The ego trip isn't the kind of trip that we like to discuss in polite company because it's fueled by pride. It's a trip that takes us to the Land of Me, Myself, and I.

Pride is an interesting word. Have you ever stopped to think that you can't say the word *pride* without saying *I*? *Pride* is the word *ride* with the letter *p* in front of it. *Pride* may be defined as "an inordinate amount of self-esteem." Its synonyms are not pretty: *egotism, vanity, conceit, arrogance, boastfulness.* Pride is puffed up, stuck up, and stiff-necked.

When we think of pride, most of us picture a loud-mouthed, ostentatious, outlandish person. In reality, some of the most prideful people are meek, mild, conservative, and calculated.

Agnes Wilson believes that pride is being "camel nosed." I have ridden a camel and I agree. A camel struts around as if to say, "I'm big, I'm bad, and my nose is beautiful." But a camel's nose is far from that—the sight of a camel's nose dripping mucus is disgusting and ugly. Proud people think they are wonders to behold. To others, however, they are ugly in their pride.

Pride blinds itself to its own presence, but it leaps up everywhere in our lives—it has a cup of coffee with us in the morning, and it puts us to bed at night. It is the forerunner of all sins, and it makes all other deadly sins even deadlier. Pride puts its me-first spin on all other sins:

- "I'm not proud; I'm just self-confident."

- "I'm not angry; I'm just emotional."

- "I'm not envious; I just want what's coming to me."

- "I'm not slothful; I'm just laid-back."

- "I'm not lustful; I'm just a red-blooded American."

- "I'm not gluttonous; I just enjoy good food."

- "I'm not greedy; I just like nice things."

Pride whispers to the overspender, "You deserve it. Even though your two credit cards are maxed out, you deserve this. Other people have as much debt as you have or more. You're not in that bad of shape. Come on, buy it."

Pride whispers to the alcoholic or drug addict, "You can stop whenever you feel like it. Just have another margarita. Do a little bit more cocaine. Smoke a little more dope. You can stop whenever you want."

Pride says to the controller, "If you don't orchestrate other people's lives, who will?"

Pride says to the blamer, "It's your parents' fault. It's your coach's fault back in junior high school. It's your boss's fault. It's your ex-spouse's fault."

Pride. It puts self on a pedestal.

Self can do anything. Self deserves things. Self has power. Self makes things happen. Self is never at fault.

Self, self, self. That's pride.

TRUE OR FALSE SELF-ESTEEM?

You might be saying, "Now, Ed, time-out. I thought as a Christian, I was supposed to have good self-esteem and a good self-concept. I thought I was supposed to think well of myself."

Absolutely. The Bible says we are to have proper self-esteem and take pride in ourselves *if our reasons are from God's Word.*

If we see ourselves the way God sees us, we should take pride in what we do, and we should have a proper self-concept. But the moment we fail to see ourselves the way God sees us, we are into an ego trip through a universe called me.

There are those who teach self-esteem and say, "You need to do whatever makes you feel good about yourself." Well, just feeling good about yourself can include a multitude of sins. A person can feel good about himself in a state of intoxication, self-indulgence, or rebellion. The pride ride is all about feeling good about self.

The way we feel about ourselves is not a measure of anything. In the first place, feelings come and go. The way we feel one day is not the way we feel the next. And in the second place, feelings are based to a great degree on external circumstances. If somebody looks at us funny or speaks sharply to us, we feel bad. If a total stranger compliments us in the elevator, we feel good. The person who bases his life solely on feeling good about himself is going to be on an unending roller coaster.

To understand pride, we have to go—in the words of ESPN sports commentator Chris Berman—back, back, back, back, back. We need to go back before Adam and Eve to see a being named Lucifer. We know him today as Satan.

Lucifer started the pride ride. He took the first ego trip into a universe named for himself. Listen to his boasts:

> I will ascend into heaven,
> I will exalt my throne above the stars of God;
> I will also sit on the mount of the congregation
> On the farthest sides of the north;
> I will ascend above the heights of the clouds,
> I will be like the Most High. (Isa. 14:13–14)

I will . . . I will . . . I will . . . I will . . . I will . . . I will. Five times, this me-istic being named Lucifer tried to elevate himself above God. He was on a pride ride, an ego trip. And God cast him from His presence.

When Satan fell from God's presence, he took with him other rebellious beings that we know as demons.

Lucifer convinced Adam and Eve to take the pride ride. His foremost temptation to them was this: "You will not surely die. For God knows that in the day you eat of it your eyes will be opened, and you will be like God, knowing good and evil" (Gen. 3:4–5).

Note the parallel. Lucifer said, "I will be like the Most High." He told Adam and Eve, "You will be like God." His words are the very essence of pride: "I can be like God. I can make my own decisions, my own judgments, my own laws and rules. I can live by my own standards and self-determine my own consequences." It was a lie then, and it is a lie now.

When A & E (Adam and Eve) took the pride ride, they took all of us as their heirs along with them. We human beings have been struggling with pride ever since.

PRIDE PUSHES US FROM GOD

There are several ways you can know whether you are on the pride ride. The first sign is this: The pride ride distances you from God.

Little Interest in Worshiping God

If you have a lack of interest in worshiping God, you are probably on a pride ride. If your schedule, your dating life, your vacation plans, or your activities are more important than your worshiping God, you are into worshiping your *self*. In Psalm 138:6, we read,

> Though the LORD is on high,
> Yet He regards the lowly;
> But the proud He knows from afar.

The prideful person isn't close to God and doesn't choose to make time for God. Pride causes a person to kick God out of the Oval Office of his life.

Me-istic Prayers

A second way to know whether you are distant from God is to take a look at your prayers.

When I was seventeen, I began keeping a prayer journal. I encourage you to write out your prayers and to keep a prayer journal—it's a great way to be specific in your prayers and also a way to confront your pride.

About a month ago, I was looking through one of my journals to see if I could spot any trends, and I noticed that my prayers were beginning to resemble a shopping list: "God help me, God bless me, God give me . . ." I realized that my prayers were becoming me-istic. I was slipping into a pride vessel and starting to embark on an ego trip.

I challenge you to spend at least one-third of your prayer time in adoration—to worship the Almighty because of His wisdom, His omniscience, His presence, and His love. Praise Him for who He is. Thank Him for what He has done. Make your prayers about God, not just yourself.

Lack of Involvement in Hands-On Ministry

One of the most important things you can do is to take an internal inventory of what you are making a priority in your life.

Take a specific look at your involvement in a local church. People who are humble are involved in ministry. They are engaged and immersed in hands-on, one-on-one ministry. Those who are prideful say that they are "above all that," that they are on another level in which direct ministry is not required.

The disciples were walking with Jesus one day, arguing about which of them would be the greatest. Jesus overheard their conversation and said to them, "If you want to become great, become a servant." You would think that the disciples, of all people, would have understood His point. But they didn't get it.

A week later, just seven days after that minisermon from Jesus, the disciples were at dinner. At that time, it was really important to have your feet washed before dinner. The people wore sandals and their feet became very dirty. Dining was done in a semireclining position, so that one person's feet could be almost in another person's face. Dirty, smelly feet don't mix well with good food.

No servant was present at the meal to wash the feet of Jesus or the disciples. And no disciple took the initiative to wash his own or anyone else's feet. So what did Jesus do? He got up and set aside His garment and put on the garment of a servant and washed the disciples' feet, one by one.

I have to admit that there are times in my life when I have been prideful, just like the disciples. I have reclined, kicked back, and been concerned only about myself. I have been too prideful to serve my wife, too prideful to help my daughter with her homework—and I have missed an opportunity to serve. I have missed opportunities to show the authentic message of Jesus Christ to those I love the most.

How about you? What opportunities have you missed?

One day we will stand before holy God, and He will ask how involved we were in His ministry and how engaged we were in His Church. Many of us will have to hang our heads in shame because we just kicked back with dirty feet and failed to serve others.

Lack of Appreciation for God's Workmanship

Another sign of the pride ride is a lack of appreciation for God's workmanship.

Often in our lives, we will win something, get a promotion, have a creative idea, or give a good talk, and we will think, *I did it. I'm so tenacious, so disciplined, so creative. I am such a leader! I have such a winsome personality! I'm something else!* Who is getting the credit? How does this make God feel? In truth, God is the One who gives us the ability and the drive to do the things we do. He is the One who has blessed us. Because of His grace, we are who we are and where we are and what we are; if there is anything good at all, it comes from His hand.

The Israelites faced this. Moses called all the Israelites together for a pregame pep talk as they were preparing to enter the promised land, the land of milk and honey. And here is what God essentially said through Moses' voice box: "Men and women, boys and girls, you are going to be blessed in the promised land. You will live in bigger houses. Your herds will increase. Your gold and silver will multiply. Life will be phenomenal for you." But then God said to them:

Beware that . . . you say in your heart, "My power and the might of my hand have gained me this wealth" . . . You shall remember the LORD your God, for it is He who gives you power to get wealth . . . If you by any means forget the LORD your God, and follow other gods, and serve them and worship them . . . you shall surely perish. (Deut. 8:11, 17–19)

That's pretty radical, but as I said, the pride ride is fatal. Who is getting the credit in your life? The answer is not in who you *say* gets the credit as much as it is in how you live your life.

PRIDE DISTANCES US FROM OTHERS

Not only does pride distance you from God, but it distances you from others. How do you know whether you are distant from others? You can look for several indicators.

If you are not being open and honest with others, you are distancing yourself from them. Pride hinders you from being openhearted.

Suppose someone hurts you—I mean really stabs you in the back. Most likely you will put some distance between yourself and that person. In most cases, you are likely to say that the other person needs to begin the reconciliation process since, after all, the other person started the pain. The Bible says, though, that the moment we receive Christ,

19

we are given the ministry of reconciliation. We are to take the initiative in restoring a broken relationship.

What did Jesus do? The Bible says that while we were yet sinners, Christ died for us. Jesus didn't wait for us to seek Him. He didn't say, "Well, I'll wait for humanity to make the first move, and then I'll talk about reconciliation." No. Jesus took the initiative and did the work to bridge the gap.

Marriages are destroyed, relationships are fragmented, and businesses are messed up today because of pride. Pride dominates us so that we white-knuckle the throttle on our pride vessel and refuse to let go of our hurt and make the first move toward reconciliation. Pride keeps us from being openhearted toward others.

Manipulation

Another way to know whether you are distancing yourself from others is to take an objective look at the way you relate to others and to ask yourself, *Am I using people to make myself look better?*

For example, some parents seek to elevate themselves by elevating their children. They are determined in their insistence that their children produce athletically, academically, and socially. A "B" isn't good enough. Second-string is unacceptable. Failures in public bring about hard, unloving responses. Why? Because these parents want their children to be perfect for one main reason—so *they* will look better as parents.

Conversations That Create Distance

At times when we are prideful, we distance people by our conversation. About a year ago on a trip I met a man who was very talented and brilliant, with a lot of potential. But I have never heard anyone talk about himself as much as this guy did in the three hours I was with him. He was unbelievable. He took pride to another level. If I had brought up the topic of aluminum siding, he probably would have told me he knew the guy who invented it.

This man had a great deal to offer the world, but people ran from him. They distanced themselves from him because of his pride. And the saddest part is, I don't even think the guy knew what he was doing. I almost wanted to say to him, "Shut up for a minute." Since he is a lot bigger than I am, I didn't do that, and I'm certainly not advocating that you tell a boastful, prideful person to keep quiet. The fact is, you need to look in the mirror and ask, "Does my conversation revolve around me, myself, and I? Am I distancing myself from people because I talk only about myself?"

FIRST-CLASS PASSENGERS ON THE PRIDE RIDE

Let's take a look at the people who ride in the first-class compartment of the pride-ride vessel—the people sitting on the other side of the curtain on the ego trip.

They are people you probably know, but perhaps by another name.

Velma Vanity

Velma Vanity is extremely concerned about her appearance. She always has a mirror in front of her face. Everything about her appearance must be just right for her to feel good about herself, and she tends to look down on others who don't have the same concern for their appearance. She is quick to notice if things aren't A-OK in their lives.

Not only does she desire for her "look" to be perfect, but she requires the same thing of those who are in close association with her, such as her spouse and her children.

Her justification, of course, is that she "just wants to look nice." Pride, however, takes "look nice" to the level of "be perfect." It's entirely acceptable for a person to want to look his best or to act in a polite way toward others. Pride requires a person to be perfect in appearance and behavior and to be the most beautiful or handsome person in any group.

Eddie Education

Eddie Education is always "degree dropping"—giving his academic credentials or the status of the schools he attended. He frequently lets others know that he has all the necessary degrees—M.B.A., D.Min., Ph.D., and A.B.C.D. E.F.G. And all from prestigious schools, of course. He might be overheard saying, "Oh, you didn't know that?

Heh, heh, heh—I thought that was common knowledge. Back when I was at my Ivy League college, we . . ."

There's nothing wrong with getting a good education or with completing all of the degrees necessary for a person to accomplish what God has called him to do in his life. Pride takes over when a person seeks to use knowledge as a tool to exalt himself in any relationship or to manipulate others to follow his point of view.

Anna Accomplishment

Anna Accomplishment has awards, titles, and honors pinned all over her. They line the walls and fill the shelves of her life so that others can see her achievements, comment on them, and hold her in higher regard. Her accomplishments give her status and are the basis for her identity.

Again, there's nothing wrong with achievement. We are to live honorable lives and do our best at all things, and when we truly have developed our talents and abilities, we are likely to receive recognition. We cross the line into pride when we look to our accomplishments as a means of elevating ourselves above others so that we can exert power or control over them. Pride is present when we look to our achievements as a justification for thinking ourselves better, more important, or of greater value than another person.

Ronny Reverse

At first glance, Ronny Reverse may look out of place in the first-class section of the pride vessel. He likely is dressed a bit shabbily and has a slouch to his shoulders. He is a reverse snob.

While it is fairly obvious that Velma, Eddie, and Anna think more highly of themselves than they ought to think, Ronny takes a different tack. He puts down the upper class as well as those who are concerned about appearance, have advanced degrees, or win awards. He is middle class and proud of it!

Ronny actually thinks of himself as a better person than those he criticizes. He sees himself as being more compassionate, more "real," more caring, more in touch with what is important. The pride element here is rooted in the word *more*. He sees himself as *better* than others, having *more* of the stuff that really matters.

Ned Name-Dropper

Ned Name-Dropper is quick to mention the name of a celebrity, athlete, or power broker. Ned wants everybody around him to know that he associates with successful and important people. He is always ready to name his closest rich and famous friend, even if it is the cousin of the best friend of his mechanic! Ned isn't in the limelight, but he wants others to think that he's only one step from it.

Martha and Marvin Materialism

Martha Materialism wouldn't dream of wearing something without a designer label. Her world revolves around the acquisition of only the best and most stylish things—and preferably the highest-quality gizmo or object that reflects the current style or fad. She is likely to ask you, "Is that Ralph Lauren or Donna Karan? Did you get that at Neiman's or Nordstrom's? Have you test-driven the new Porsche?"

Martha is married to another passenger in the pride-ride vehicle: Marvin Materialism. He lets you know the current status of his investments and the amount he has accumulated in his estate. He routinely talks in terms of "six figures" and "seven figures" and delights in identifying the address of his place of business and the fact that he has a corner office on the top floor.

What Fuels Your Behavior?

Pride fuels the behaviors manifested by Velma Vanity, Eddie Education, Anna Accomplishment, Ronny Reverse, Ned Name-Dropper, and Martha and Marvin Materialism. Each person looks to something other than their relationship with God to provide a feeling of self-worth.

Sadly, few in the first-class section of this pride-ride vehicle are smiling. Appearance, degrees, possessions, affiliations, accomplishments, and even snobbish put-downs of others can never give a person a genuine feeling of self-worth or joy. Pride is always empty. It is based on things that do not last and are not of God; therefore, it is based on things that do not satisfy the deepest needs of the human heart.

Pride and deep inner peace cannot coexist. Pride always produces frustration, a lack of contentment. The prideful person is always looking for something more to build himself up to yet a higher plateau. He is always looking to the world around him for identity and validation. Those who have genuine inner peace look to God and draw from their relationship with Him all the identity and validation they need.

What Can You Do About Your Pride?

What can you do to remove the poison of pride from your life?

For most people, the first step is actually to recognize pride. We are amazingly blind to our pride. We rarely audit our behavior, listen to what we say, or take the time to think about our attitudes.

You must put your seat and table into an upright, locked position and prepare for a landing. You need to throttle back, land, taxi to the gate, and exit the pride plane. Then as you walk through the airport, you need to do something really radical—you need to strip.

Stay with me. You need to take off all of this prideful stuff you are wearing as garments and clothe yourself with a true biblical fashion statement. First Peter 5:5 gives the instruction to "be clothed with humility."

I love what Peter Wiersby says about humility. He says that humility is not demeaning yourself—that is *false* humility. True humility is not thinking of yourself at all. The authentic humble person becomes so other-centered that he doesn't worry about himself. We are told,

God resists the proud,
But gives grace to the humble. (1 Peter 5:5)

How do you put on humility in a practical way?

First, you must confess your pride to God and ask Him to cleanse you of it. Then, you must discipline yourself to spend time each day in worship of God. When you see yourself as a finite human being standing in the presence of the Almighty, you cannot help being humbled. You can't stand beside the cradle of Jesus and be proud. You can't stand beside the carpenter bench of Jesus and pump out your chest. You can't stand beside the One who was a friend of prostitutes, tax collectors, and sinners and still be stuck-up. You can't stand beside the cross on Golgotha and remain proud. The Bible tells you that Jesus was rich, but He became poor for your sake. He laid aside all kinds of stuff to put on the garment of a servant. And that is what you must do.

Second, you must begin to thank God and to appreciate His workmanship. Yes, take a compliment and say "Thank you" when people applaud you, but remember always who gave you the power to earn, achieve, attain, or acquire. Remember who blessed you. Remember who gave you the windfall. God did!

Third, you must be engaged and immersed in the hands-on ministry of a local church. You must seek ways to serve others.

The most potent way I know to confront pride and eradicate it from your life is to get involved in a ministry outreach *to the very person, or type of person, that you like the least.* Complete this sentence: "I would never want to be _____." You have just identified the person or group of people to whom you should minister. If you'd never want to be a homeless person, a drug addict, an unwed mother, a paraplegic, a mean older person, a resident in a nursing home—whatever the classification of people you name—that is your prime mission field if you truly want to get pride out of your life.

Tough medicine? Yes. But pride is often a very tough root to pull out of our souls.

Don't Let Pride Keep You Out

A tragic element of the pride ride is that it distances you from God and others in this life, and it can distance you from God and others for all eternity. Pride keeps scores and scores of people from having a personal relationship with Jesus Christ. Pride keeps you believing that if you just live a good life on this earth, if you are sincere, if you believe whatever you believe with a strong belief, you will get into heaven.

The Bible says you are saved by grace, which is the unmerited favor you receive from God. You are saved through *faith* in the Lord Jesus Christ, not your works. There is nothing you can say or do to earn, win, or achieve your salvation. What is required is that you admit your pride, ask Jesus to come into your life as your Savior, and then seek to live out what He wants for you, not what you want for yourself.

ABSOLUTELY NO UPSIDE

Are there any good benefits to pride? No. None.

Any benefits a prideful person may experience are going to be extremely short-term and temporary. There are no long-term and lasting benefits to a prideful attitude. There certainly are no eternal benefits.

Pride is deadly in all of its manifestations. It kills you spiritually, emotionally, physically; and it kills your relationships, your influence, your integrity, and your witness for Christ. It can kill your future in eternity.

How about it? Isn't it time you landed your vessel and got off the pride ride? Isn't it time you quit taking the ego trip? Isn't it about time you clothed yourself with humility?

ANGER

Harnessing the Heat

I'm chapped."

"That really hacks me off."

Or as my uncle from Laurel, Mississippi, says, "That gives me the reds, son."

These expressions and others describe an emotion that is central to human nature, far-reaching, and complex.

Anger is everywhere. It is a bad but frequent guest in our homes. It rides in our cars especially, it seems, on certain freeways. It enters our bedrooms uninvited. It joins our foursome on the golf course. It rears its head in our relationships with our children. It sits beside us at work. And it stands close to us as we wait our turn behind a person with too many items in the express line at the supermarket.

Not only is anger one of the most common of the fatal distractions, but it is a sin many people enjoy. They like blowing off steam, venting, or licking their wounds and thinking up means of revenge.

A number of social commentators have used the phrase "age of rage" to describe our society, and I whole-heartedly agree with them. We live in an age of pipe bombs, drive-by shootings, battered women, and movie heroes who bear "lethal weapons" and "die hard." It's easy to dream of running away to a distant deserted island to escape the anger all around us, but the Bible tells us that we are to influence others for the kingdom of God—even in the age of rage.

Anger is an emotion that has many physical manifes-tations: our blood pressure rises, our mouths get dry, our fists clench, our muscles tense automatically, our adrena-line begins to flow freely. We feel ready to fight. What we do with our anger tells a lot about us.

THE WAYS WE EXPRESS ANGER

The Toxic Waste Approach

Some people handle anger as if they are dealing with toxic waste. They bury it deep within themselves and pre-sent an A-OK outward appearance. But over the years, the anger begins to leak out and contaminate them. It enters the stream of their thoughts and causes them to be sick. Unresolved anger can impact their attitudes, relationships, and ultimately their faith. Are you harboring any toxic waste of anger inside you?

The Volcano Approach

Some deal with anger like a volcano.

One day when I took my kids swimming, there was a ball in the pool, just floating around. I wanted to show my kids a trick. I took the ball with one hand and pushed it under the surface of the pool. After about ten seconds, it was hard to keep it there. The ball suddenly blew up from underneath my hand and went up about four feet in the air. The kids said, "Wow, Daddy, unbelievable!"

Anger works that way. It can come up without any warning. You can be in a great mood when you leave home, but then the moment someone cuts you off on the freeway, there it is. You can be humming along at work, but then comes *that* phone call that causes the steam inside you to vent.

Volcanic people can rumble and rumble for days, weeks, and even years. Then the day comes when they say to themselves, *I've been taking this for five years, and I'm not going to take it anymore. I'm going to give that person who made me angry a piece of my mind.* And they spew the hot lava and burning ash of their anger all over another person, leaving behind only the charred remains of a relationship. Volcanic people never apologize for being angry—which is one reason they are like volcanoes.

The Snow Cone Approach

Others express anger like a snow cone. When they become upset, they immediately turn on the big chill. They give the person who has wronged them an ice-cold shoulder, and the icicles virtually drip off the eaves of their words: "No, nothing's wrong. No. Nothing. Really."

The Microwave Approach

And finally some people express anger like a microwave oven. They confront a situation that angers them with a near instantaneous response. It's almost as if you can hear the ten-second time-cook button go *beep . . . beep . . . beep . . . BAM!* They explode. Those who have a short fuse are often set off by things that others find minor in nature. Their anger is just below the surface at all times.

How do *you* express anger?

IS ALL ANGER BAD?

One reason we may fail to see anger as a fatal distraction in our lives is that anger can have a good side to it. In fact, Ephesians 4:26 starts out, "Be angry."

God gave us emotions for a reason. Anger should be

our automatic response anytime we are confronted with something that is evil or unjust. We should feel a little blood-boiling when we see abused children, starved people, or innocent people suffering because of another person's power trip. Our anger should motivate us to take positive action. In its purest form, anger is a trigger that ignites our passion and causes us to react to situations around us.

There is nothing wrong with anger itself. Anger is neutral. It's a little like a crowbar. A crowbar can be used in a very positive way—for example, to open a window that is stuck. It can also be used to break in the window of a home in order to rob it or bash in the head of a person in order to harm that person. The crowbar is not the issue. In these cases, the purpose for using the crowbar is the issue.

You can determine whether anger is a fatal distraction for you by answering this question: What causes me to feel angry? Take a look at the things you choose to get angry about.

When I was a sophomore at Florida State University, I took a biology test and scored a whopping 68. I was not happy. I said, "This makes me angry. I'm going to ace the next test." And sure enough, with a little help from my then girlfriend and study partner, and now wife, Lisa, I got an A on that next biology test. I focused my anger on a good cause in a positive way.

If you are a salesperson and suddenly someone seems to steal your major account right out from under you, anger might be a very good response. Not anger at the person who took the account, but anger at yourself for having become a bit lackadaisical. Anger can cause you to work harder.

WHAT MAKES THE LORD ANGRY?

Some people are convinced that Christians should never get angry. They think believers should show only love, joy, peace, forgiveness, and a kum-ba-yah attitude twenty-four hours a day, seven days a week. Although these are traits of believers, the Bible says that believers are to get angry from time to time.

Scripture plainly reveals that God got angry. "The anger of the Lord" is a phrase that appears eighteen times in the Old Testament.

Jesus became angry in a positive way and for good reasons. When Jesus discovered that the temple was being turned into a mall, He became angry, and His anger motivated Him to take action. He did not walk up and gently say, "Hey, guys, you ought not to do what you are doing. It's not a good idea because, after all, this is My Father's house." No! Read what He did:

He found in the temple those who sold oxen and sheep and doves, and the money changers doing business. When He had made a whip of cords, He drove them all out of the temple, with the sheep and the oxen, and poured out the changers' money and overturned the tables. And He said to those who sold doves, "Take these things away! Do not make My Father's house a house of merchandise!" (John 2:14–16)

Later, when the disciples reflected on Jesus' actions, they recalled a line from Psalm 69, and they perceived that Jesus had demonstrated this concept: "Zeal for Your house has eaten Me up" (John 2:17; Ps. 69:9). Jesus' anger motivated Him to set things right in the temple.

In another instance, Jesus confronted the scribes and Pharisees. As you read what Jesus said to them in Matthew 23, you can almost hear the sting of anger in His voice. He said, "Woe to you, scribes and Pharisees!" He called them hypocrites, blind guides, and murderers of the prophets. His anger motivated Him to speak the truth.

WHEN SHOULD WE BE ANGRY?

Anytime God's will and God's Word are maligned, we should get angry.

Anytime we see a person who knows Christ personally begin to thumb his nose in God's face, spin on his heels, and do his own thing—choosing to live in sin when he knows better—we should get angry.

Anytime we see people treated badly because of their

looks, the color of their skin, or their socioeconomic level, we should get angry.

Anytime we see parents exasperating or abusing their children, we should get angry.

These are all things that make God angry, and the things that anger God should anger us.

WHY IS ANGER SO DEADLY?

If anger has a good side to it, how can we tell when we are dealing with anger that is deadly to our souls? Let me summarize when anger is a fatal distraction.

First, when negative outbursts of anger threaten to kill relationships we value, that anger is a fatal distraction.

Second, when anger is allowed to fester and thoughts of revenge seem to consume us, that anger is a fatal distraction.

Third, when anger keeps us from forgiving others, that anger is a fatal distraction.

HOW, THEN, ARE WE TO EXPRESS ANGER?

Earlier, I quoted the first part of Ephesians 4:26, "Be angry." The key to that verse lies in the second half: "And do not sin." We must always keep in mind this balance: *We must not sin in our anger.*

I believe some Bible analogies help us better understand how anger operates and how we can keep from sinning in anger.

A Trapeze

Have you ever watched a circus trapeze artist soar over an obstacle or fly through a ring of fire? That often happens with anger. Anger is usually not the first emotion that most of us feel in response to a bad situation. Generally we have other emotions as a first response, but we "trapeze" over or through those emotions and find ourselves landing in a spot called anger.

Jacob had twelve sons. He loved them all, but he had a favorite son: Joseph. Joseph was the apple of his eye. He gave Joseph the family's designer robe. And the reactions from the other brothers included hatred, hurt, and rejection. Their self-esteem took a hit. But instead of dealing with their feelings of jealousy, hurt, and rejection, they immediately jumped on an emotional trapeze and soared over those emotions and landed in anger. In their anger, they tossed Joseph into a pit and then sold him into slavery.

Why do we soar over the real emotions we feel? Because anger is usually easier and quicker to express. Emotions such as jealousy, rejection, and hurt feelings are harder to define and more difficult to work through.

Let me give you an example of how this works in our world today. A man may call his wife from work to say, "I'll be home at six o'clock." His wife decides to make an extra-special dinner and plans to have it ready when he walks in the door at six o'clock. At six-thirty, he isn't home. At six-forty-five, he still isn't home. To make matters far worse, he has a mobile phone, and he hasn't called. Her dinner is overcooked and cold. She's upset. She's hurt. She's disappointed.

What happens when this man walks in the door a few minutes after seven o'clock? His wife trapezes over these initial emotions and blasts him with an Uzi round of shots: "You are *always* late. You *never* keep your word. You *never* show me any consideration. You *always* take me for granted. You have ruined a perfectly good dinner. You can just eat what's left by yourself!" *Bam, bam, bam, bam, bam.* The evening is killed, and the relationship has some holes that need to be patched up.

Are you using anger today as a way of avoiding or leaping over the real emotions you should face? Are you trying to avoid certain issues in your life and resorting to anger instead?

A Bed

A second insight into anger is found in Ephesians 4:26, "Do not let the sun go down on your wrath." Anger is like a lumpy bed.

Have you ever thought to yourself, *I'm angry, but if I just get a little shut-eye, I'll feel better in the morning?* That's rarely the case. The anger doesn't go away. Instead, it intensifies overnight. Whatever made you angry is turned over and over on the rotisserie grill of your heart and mind all night long. The juices of anger poison your attitude so that you rarely wake up singing when the alarm goes off. Instead, you wake up growling. If you continue to go to bed with the same unresolved issue night after night, the anger only grows.

Years ago when I did marriage counseling, I advised every young couple I saw to adopt the sunset principle. I said, "Anytime you see the beautiful Texas sunset, think about your relationship. If you have any problem with your spouse, choose to resolve it before you go to bed that night. Do what it takes to bring the issue to a peaceful resolution."

Every time I have slept in anger I have put distance between Lisa and me. There have been times when we have stayed up until three o'clock in the morning to resolve an issue between us so that we wouldn't go to bed with anger. Were we tired the rest of the day? Yes. But we were at peace. And friend, waking up a little tired physically but in peace emotionally with a person you love is far better than waking up physically rested but with turmoil inside.

If you go to bed in anger, I don't believe you *can* wake up fully rested physically. You may put in the hours of snooze time, but your body never fully relaxes to take full benefit of it. I advise people with sleep problems to take stock of their anger level. Are you upset with someone? Are you upset about what somebody has done to you? Are you angry about a situation? Are you angry at life in general? Are you angry at God?

When I think about going to bed in anger, I think about Jonah, the quintessential pouting prophet. He walked out of his house one day, and God spoke to his heart, "Jonah, go to Nineveh, that wicked, fortified city, and preach My forgiveness and love. The Ninevites matter to Me" (see Jonah 1:2).

Jonah opted not to go. He basically said, "No way. I am not going to deal with those people. They are our archenemies, and they are in the process of invading Israel and doing all kinds of nasty things to us Israelites. God, You should nuke them, not forgive them. They're bad people!"

We all know the story—how Jonah decided to take a Mediterranean cruise rather than go to Nineveh and how God created a giant fish to swallow Jonah after the sailors threw him overboard. Once those digestive juices began to do their work on Jonah, he had a change of heart. He said, "I will pay what I have vowed. Salvation is of the LORD" (Jonah 2:9). He agreed to do things God's way.

When Jonah preached in Nineveh, a revival broke out. A million Ninevites repented and turned to God. God was happy. The Ninevites were high-fiving each other. But Jonah was angry. He couldn't believe that God would save the people. He still wanted God to destroy them, regardless of their repentance.

Jonah went to bed with anger, and he turned his anger over and over and over again on the rotisserie grill of his mind. He said to God, "Please take my life from me, for it is better for me to die than to live!" (Jonah 4:3). And that's how the story ends: Jonah wanted to die in his anger, and God saved the Ninevites.

Are you holding on to anger—even to your grave? If you are angry about any issue that does not also anger God, your anger is unfounded. Let it go! If you make anger your bed, you will not be able to rise from it to do all that God has designed and planned for you to do in your life.

A Door

Paul wrote to the Ephesians, "Do not let the sun go down on your wrath, nor give place to the devil" (Eph. 4:26–27). In one translation, we read, "When you are angry you give a mighty foothold to the devil" (TLB). In another, we find, "Do not give the devil an opportunity" (NASB).

When I was growing up, my father seemed to me to be paranoid about mosquitoes. It could be fifteen degrees outside, but if I came home and let the door stand open for five extra seconds, I'd hear my father say, "Close that door right now! Mosquitoes!" To this day, my father can't stand open doors.

How often do we open the door to anger—thinking we are doing nothing wrong—and give the devil an opportunity to enter?

Anger always runs with a rough crowd. When we talk about the attitude of inner-city gangs, we often say they are angry. When we describe murderers and terrorists, the word *anger* comes to mind. A primary word we use to describe those who abuse and batter their spouses and children is *angry*. Anger plays a role in nearly all crimes. It has been that way from the beginning.

Cain and Abel were brothers. Both took offerings to the Lord—God accepted Abel's offering but rejected Cain's offering. Cain was jealous and felt hatred for his brother and rejection from God. Rather than deal with those emotions, he jumped on the trapeze and landed in the waiting arms of anger.

The Bible reports, "Cain was very angry, and his countenance fell" (Gen. 4:5). If you had been there, you would have had no problem telling that Cain was upset—anger was written all over his face.

God was more than willing to give Cain another chance. He said to Cain, "Why are you angry? And why has your countenance fallen? If you do well, will you not be accepted? And if you do not do well, sin lies at the door. And its desire is for you, but you should rule over it" (Gen. 4:6–7).

What a powerful message this is, and yet we so often pass right over it! God said to Cain, "You have a choice. You can face up to what is really bothering you and set things right. Or you can open the door to anger and invite it in." Cain invited anger in, and his anger led to murder.

Anger runs with a friend named revenge. If you open the door to anger, revenge nearly always tags along. How many people today are spending their time, energy, and effort to get back at someone who hurt them? They say to themselves, *I'll get back at that coach. I'll get back at my mom. I'll get back at my ex-spouse. I'll get back at my boss.*

The Lord commands: "Never take your own revenge, beloved, but leave room for the wrath of God, for it is written, 'VENGEANCE IS MINE, I WILL REPAY,' says the Lord" (Romans 12:19 NASB). Allow God to deal with the situation. Let it go. Not only will you be doing the right thing for your enemy, but you will also be doing the right thing for yourself. Rather than open the door to the devil in your anger, choose to open the door to the Lord so that He can do His work.

A Sword

Have you ever said things in anger that you wished you could take back? Proverbs 12:18 describes the situation: "There is one who speaks like the piercings of a sword." In today's movie culture, the sting of the tongue might be compared to a light saber.

Why are words such a powerful weapon? Because the wounds inflicted by a sword heal, but the wounds inflicted by words remain alive in the memory forever. Once hurtful words are spoken, the other person is gashed and slashed in a way that never fully heals.

In Ephesians 4:29 we read, "Let no corrupt word proceed out of your mouth, but what is good for necessary edification, that it may impart grace to the hearers." In Proverbs 12:18, we also find this admonition: "The tongue of the wise promotes health."

Years ago, when we had small babies, Lisa put all of the children's pacifiers into a pot of boiling water, intending to sterilize them. She forgot the boiling Binkeys, however, and when the water boiled out, they caught on fire. You have never in your life smelled anything as bad as Binkey smoke. It permeated our house and kept us out of our kitchen for at least forty-eight hours. James told us that the tongue is like a fire (James 3:6). It leaves a stench worse than Binkey smoke.

How Can You Rule Over Anger?

Knowing how anger works is one thing. Dealing with it is another. The Bible tells us, "Let all bitterness, wrath, anger, clamor, and evil speaking be put away from you" (Eph. 4:31). In other words, do the following:

- Get off the trapeze. Deal with the primary emotional issues that you are overlooking or stuffing away.

- Refuse to allow anger to build up inside you by not going to bed with it—deal with it!

- Seek God's forgiveness for the anger you are harboring against Him and against others. Slam the door on the devil and on all thoughts of revenge.

- Lay down the sword of your tongue. Choose to

speak words that build up rather than tear down others.

Is it easy to rule over anger? No.
Is it possible? Yes!
Let me also offer several specific and practical things you can do in any particular situation to harness the heat of anger.

Ask for God's Help

A forgiving spirit is at the heart of your ability to rule over anger. Ask the Lord to help you forgive the person who has hurt you or rejected you. Ask Him to help you control your anger. Ask Him to help you deal with the things that cause you to be angry.

THE A-N-G-E-R APPROACH

Affirm the Relationship

Let the other person know, "I value you. I value our relationship." Before you confront any issues that may lie between you and another person, assure the other person of your love, concern, care, or feelings of worthiness. If it's a work situation, say, "I value my job. I enjoy working here. This position means a lot to me." If it's a personal relationship, say, "You mean a lot to me, and I know our relationship means even more to a holy God."

Negotiate with "I Feel" Statements

Two words that should be avoided in situations related to anger are *never* and *always*. They are like gasoline on an emotional fire. Rather than accuse the other person with blanket statements, make your statements in terms of "I feel." Let the other person know, "I feel hurt. I feel rejected. I feel ignored."

Guard the Volume Level

If your tone of voice is loud, you are going to be perceived to be angry even if you aren't. Turn down the volume of your voice. Speak in a tender tone of voice—not syrupy sweet, cynical, or sarcastic in its kindness, but genuinely gentle. Proverbs 15:1 sums it up: "A soft answer turns away wrath, but a harsh word stirs up anger."

Establish Resolve

Determine what both of you can do to make certain a situation that generated anger does not occur again. Can you call? Can you budget? Can you reschedule? Can you reprioritize? If the other person will not negotiate with you and rejects your efforts, shake the dust off your shoes, and move on. If you are in a marriage and your spouse refuses to address certain issues, seek help. Refuse to accept anger as the status quo.

Release the Other Person Fully

Releasing others from the hurt that resulted in your anger is not necessarily a onetime event. You may need to pray a number of times for the grace of God to forgive another person. If so, keep praying!

If you continue to hold bitterness, hatred, resentment, or anger against another person, your relationship with God is going to be hindered. Jesus taught clearly, "For if you forgive men their trespasses, your heavenly Father will also forgive you. But if you do not forgive men their trespasses, neither will your Father forgive your trespasses" (Matt. 6:14–15). As long as you hold on to another person's fault against you in a spirit of anger and unforgiveness, your anger cannot be quenched, and your own sins cannot be forgiven. Ask God to help you forgive fully.

CHOOSE TO RULE OVER YOUR ANGER

Do not let anger rule you. It leads down a path of deadly destruction.

Choose instead to rule over your anger and to harness and channel your anger into the things that not only build up your character in Christ Jesus, but that also build up others and build up the kingdom of God.

You can do it!

ENVY

Fighting the Ugly Green-Eyed Monster

I'm intrigued by cheers. Not too long ago, I asked the people in my congregation to stand so that I could lead them in a cheer. I knew it was early, but I also knew that many of them had already had their Starbucks coffee in the church lobby and they were fired up and ready to go. Here's the cheer I taught them:

> U-G-L-Y. You ain't got no alibi.
> You're ugly . . . envy. You're ugly.

Before we finished, we had the rafters shaking. The truth is, envy is as ugly as sin because it's just that—sin.

We have associated the color green with envy. We say about a person that he is "green with envy." Green seems to be a popular color lately in the fashion world. It certainly is popular among golfers, the prestigious green jacket going to the winner of the Masters Tournament. But no person wants to be described as having a greenish tint to his skin because that means he looks sick. To be green with envy means to be so consumed with envy that one is sick at heart—and it shows! That's what makes envy so ugly. Those who have it seldom recognize it, but it is a sickness obvious to all who see it objectively.

All of the other fatal distractions have a singular opposite. For example, the opposite of pride is humility; the opposite of anger is forgiving love; the opposite of gluttony is self-control. Envy, by comparison, is opposed to all virtues. It defies everything it contacts. It desires that no good thing happen to anybody else, be owned by anybody else, or be in relationship to anybody else. It is against anything that might be considered a blessing *if that blessing is being received by someone else.*

Envy is different from the other fatal distractions in another way. Nearly all of the other fatal distractions start out with some degree of pleasure. Gluttony gives us pleasure before it turns sour. Anger gives us the pleasure of blowing up before we deal with the ruins we have created. But envy is different. It starts out bad and stays bad.

A Real Monster

It's easy to depict envy as a monster. I can imagine one with green skin, a scowl on its face, and fangs to inject poison into every person it encounters. This monster has narrow, squinty eyes that appraise what everybody else has, does, and is. It has giant ears to hear about any awards or honors that are being given to other people.

Envy is defined in one dictionary as "an evil eye." It is a sin that begins in the eyes. A partner closes a megadeal and receives a huge bonus, and your eye turns toward envy. A gorgeous woman walks into the room, and the other women in the room give her the evil eye. I personally define *envy* this way: "being sad about someone else's successes or blessings and glad about someone else's failures or troubles." Envy is a consuming desire to have every other person be as unsuccessful as you feel.

Envy seeks to level the playing field—either to level "up" self or to level "down" others. The goal is to have self emerge as number one. How is this different from pride? Pride assumes the self is already number one. Envy intuitively knows self is not number one but seeks to use every available means of getting to the *numero uno* spot.

I heard a story about an envious merchant. He was particularly envious of his number one competitor in his small town. One day as this man was walking along the beach he found a bottle. Out of the bottle emerged an I-Dream-of-Jeannie-type genie. This genie looked at the envious merchant and said, "Sir, your wish is my command. One caveat, though. Whatever you wish for, I will give in double measure to the person you envy so much." This man thought for a second and then said, "I wish to be blind in one eye."

Envy is hoping that another person will fail so that you can succeed on the back of his failure.

When I rode the bench as a basketball player at Florida State University, I struggled with envy. I had countless opportunities to watch the person who was the starting player in what I perceived to be "my" position. When he drove the lane and dunked the ball over two opposing players and the eighteen thousand fans went wild, I had a hard time clapping for him. *Yeah, well, that was an okay move.* And when he came away from a clash with another player with a slight limp, I thought, *Oh, is he hurt? Too bad. How soon can I go in?* I felt envy. And it was ugly.

OF WHOM ARE WE MOST ENVIOUS?

In my church are dozens of young men and women who are genuine go-getters and who are making a mark in their professions. More than any of the other fatal distractions, I am wary of envy as the sin that can wreak the most havoc in our church. Why? Because we tend to be envious of people who are like us and who seem to function or compete in our same arena.

Salesmen aren't envious of artists—they are envious of other salesmen who sell more than they sell. A mother doesn't envy a professional athlete—she envies other moms whose children seem to be more successful. Pastors aren't envious of real estate developers—they are envious of other pastors who seem to have larger churches, larger budgets, and higher-profile ministries.

Within the church, those who are teachers tend to be more envious of other teachers, those who are in the music ministry tend to be more envious of other musicians, and so forth.

Within our families, envy tends to manifest itself among relatives who are the most alike in their personalities and talents. Within companies, envy tends to operate most strongly among those who have similar job descriptions or who hold similar rungs on the corporate ladder.

What happens when envy begins to rule? James 3:16 tells us, "For where envy and self-seeking exist, confusion and every evil thing are there." We cast doubt about the accomplishments of others. We ridicule and reject successful people. We avoid parties and ceremonies that honor those we envy. We engage in gossip and backbiting in an attempt to dethrone the person who we perceive has become king or queen for a day.

Envy sets up a person to lie in order to get what others have and what he thinks he should have. It sets up a person to hate those who have received what he wanted for himself, but what was rightfully not his. The envious person creates a wall between himself and others—he chooses to distance himself from those who have what he wants. The envious person may eventually seek to murder the person he envies—perhaps not literally—but to destroy the career, damage prized possessions, or take actions that will tarnish the person's reputation.

In the process, what is destroyed in our souls? Our joy. Envy kills our ability to be part of the party. When we lose joy, we lose motivation and enthusiasm and hope. To live without hope is to live without a reason for getting up in the morning. It is to join the living dead. Envy consumes us at the life source of our being. It consumes us and destroys us.

Is a Little Envy Really So Vile?

Most people are quick to dismiss envy from the sin list. You may be saying right now, "Come on, Ed. A little envy is motivational. A little jealousy is part of competition. It's the way our system works."

It may be the way our system works, but it's not the way God works.

God does not distinguish bigger from lesser sins. God does not have a grocery list of sins that He prioritizes. According to the Bible, we matter so much to God that

He gave us Jesus Christ so that we might have life and have it to its fullest. The Bible also tells us that when we practice sin, our sin keeps us from experiencing life to its fullest. Envy keeps us from the life God wants us to enjoy.

Envy is listed in the New Testament with some ugly things: deceit, rudeness, murder, drunkenness, orgies, hypocrisy, slander, and stealing (Rom. 1:28–32; Titus 3:3). Solomon's words are just as true today as they were in Bible times: "A sound heart is life to the body, but envy is rottenness to the bones" (Prov. 14:30).

Few of us would place envy and murder in the same classification, or regard envy as part of evil character, but God does. Few of us regard envy as something that can kill a person, but God says that death comes to those who are filled with envy. We make a grave mistake if we dismiss envy with a smile and a shrug.

FOUR UGLY FACETS OF ENVY

If envy goes unchecked, it will have these four devastating effects:

1. Envy Damages Our Self-Esteem

Psychology Today magazine once conducted a survey of twenty-five thousand people, and the editors found that envy is the root cause of poor self-esteem. Many people deal with feelings of inferiority. But let's take a closer look at what it means to feel inferior. People feel inferior only if they compare themselves and determine that someone else is superior. We can become so preoccupied with comparing ourselves to other people and what they possess that we lose sight of who we are and what we possess.

Let me assure you, no matter how excellent you are in all ways, you can always find someone who does something better than you do it, has more of something than you have of it, or is more talented in at least one area than you are. There's always going to be somebody who is stronger, smarter, faster, richer, prettier, and bigger than you are. There's always going to be somebody who can close deals easier, sing better, act better, preach better—you name it, there's somebody who can do whatever you do and do it better in the opinion of at least one other person. Even world-class record holders find that their records are usually broken during their lifetimes and often within a few months or years.

Comparison is futile. It does not reap any benefit. It only brings about feelings of low self-esteem.

Low self-esteem causes a person to fall into a trap—usually one of these traps:

Plastic praise. This praise looks good at a glance but has very little value. Plastic praise says such things as, "Well, she does have beautiful hair, but her makeup is never applied correctly." "He's a good businessman, but honestly now, would you want to take him fishing?" "Oh, she's a great mother, but, girl, have you ever seen how she keeps her house?" Plastic praise is actually a camouflage for raw, green envy.

Mean motives. Envy often puts up a smoke screen of questions about a person's motives. Envy tries to mask itself by saying such things as, "He may be riding high in the success standings right now, but I guarantee you, he's cheating somebody somewhere." "I wonder what motivates him?" "He gave me a great gift—I wonder what he's after?"

Condescending compliments. I'm pretty good at this one. Someone may say to me, "Wow, Ed, we just got back from Hawaii, and that has to be the most beautiful place on the planet." If I'm in one of my condescending-compliment moods, I will probably retort, "Yeah, it is beautiful there, but have you seen the Cayman Islands? If you want to see beautiful, go to the Caymans." Maybe you have driven around a neighborhood with a friend, and the friend said, "That house has the most fantastic landscaping I've ever seen." Then you replied, "Yeah, it's all right, but you should see my uncle's place."

Envy fuels plastic praise, mean motives, and condescending compliments.

And what about your reading and viewing habits? Do you enjoy tabloid television programs or the gossip columns in newspapers and magazines? Both forms of "entertainment" are rooted in envy. We seem to enjoy reading about the dirty laundry and failures of others. We come away with a smug smile on our faces. We pat ourselves on the back and say, "You'd never catch me doing that"—or at least, "You'd never catch me on a television program admitting to that!" Or we want to know which movie star has how many houses and which celebrity makes how much, solely so we can say, "But I wouldn't trade places with that person for the world because he _____"—and you can fill in the blank with whatever failure or flaw you happen to know about the person.

Why do people say these things? Those who are always cutting down others, or who make sarcastic and cynical remarks about every success story they hear, nearly always have low self-esteem. They are attempting to boost their status by tearing down others.

Proverbs 27:4 asks, "Wrath is cruel and anger a torrent, but who is able to stand before jealousy?" The envious person will always find a way to bring others down to his level or ideally a degree lower than his own level.

2. *Envy Creates a Lack of Contentment*

Contentment is not something that happens to us automatically. It is something we learn. Paul wrote to the Philippians,

> I have learned in whatever state I am, to be content: I know how to be abased, and I know how to abound. Everywhere and in all things I have learned both to be

full and to be hungry, both to abound and to suffer need. I can do all things through Christ who strengthens me. (Phil. 4:11–13)

Paul was not talking about complacency. He was talking about contentment, which is being happy enough with what you have or are in any given situation. Paul learned to be content regardless of the outer conditions in which he found himself. That does not mean that Paul would have given up the chance to change some things about his circumstances. At the time he wrote this, he was under house arrest in Rome, and he certainly would have liked to change that circumstance!

Being content is not the same thing as being complacent. To be complacent is to say, "Nothing will ever change, and nothing can be done, so I'm stuck here for the rest of my life." Paul never had that attitude. He never stopped believing God for his release from prison so that he might continue to spread the good news of Jesus Christ. Paul was not complacent, but he was *content*.

How can we be content even in the midst of a circumstance we would like to change? By saying as Paul did, "I can do all things through Christ who strengthens me" (Phil. 4:13). We must acknowledge with thanksgiving and with faith that the Lord is with us and that He will provide for us all that we need in our present circumstance. With that attitude, we *can* be content with what we have, even as we wait, work, and believe for something better.

The envious person does not know contentment. He is discontent with whatever he has. He is never patient, and he never fully trusts God to work on his behalf.

Envy was at the heart of the parable Jesus told about a prodigal son. What motivated this young man in his late teens to take his dad's trust fund and go out to a "far country" and spend it all on loose living? One reason was that he didn't want to live in the shadow of his older brother. He was envious of what his brother was to inherit.

As is true in all cases, this young man discovered that you cannot outrun, outmaneuver, or outsmart sin. He eventually came back home, and his father forgave him so completely and was so excited about his return that he gave his son a major Texas-style barbecue, bought him a new wardrobe, and restored his inheritance.

The younger brother wasn't the only one in the story, however, who had envy. The major subplot of this story, which often is overlooked, is the story of what happened to the older brother. How did the older brother react to the news that his brother had returned home and had been fully forgiven?

He was eaten alive with envy. He sulked and pouted, and he refused to enter the house. When the father came out to reason with him, the older brother said, "I've been working hard and doing the right things all these years, and you haven't given me so much as a pizza party."

The father replied, "Son, you are always with me, and all that I have is yours. It was right that we should make merry and be glad, for your brother was dead and is alive again, and was lost and is found" (Luke 15:31–32).

The older brother was discontent. He had lost his joy to envy. He wasn't happy with what he had—and in reality, he hadn't lost a thing. He compared the favor and mercy shown to his brother with his feelings at that moment, and he allowed envy to rule his heart.

Are you so concerned today about what you don't have and what somebody else has that you are failing to thank God for the blessings He has bestowed on your life? Are you allowing envy to rob you of your ability to enjoy life?

3. Envy Keeps Us from Enjoying the Successes of Others

If you are envious of another person, you cannot enjoy the celebrations in his honor. A classic example is found in 1 Samuel 18.

King Saul—a decorated war hero and the ruler of the nation—became envious of a young country boy named David. Saul was not envious of David's harp-playing or songwriting ability. He wasn't jealous of David's appearance—after all, the Bible says that Saul was the most handsome guy in the land and that he stood head and shoulders taller than all of the other people in the nation (1 Sam. 9:2). He wasn't even envious of David when David killed Goliath. In fact, Saul was so pleased that David had won the battle against the giant of the Philistines that he invited him to live in the palace and be a part of his royal family.

When David began to be popular, King Saul became envious of him. After one battle against the Philistines, David and Saul returned home, and they were greeted with women who ran out singing and dancing with tambourines, saying, "Saul has slain his thousands, and David his ten thousands" (1 Sam. 18:7). Saul became very angry. He stormed in a rage, "They have ascribed to David ten thousands, and to me they have ascribed only thousands. Now what more can he have but the kingdom?" Envy filled Saul's heart. And the Bible says that from that day on, Saul "eyed David" with the evil green eyes of envy (1 Sam. 18:8–9).

Added to that was Saul's envy of David's relationship with the Lord. What a hideous form of envy—becoming envious of the ministry success of another person. When you hear about a person leading someone to Christ, what is your response? Do you rejoice that a person has found Christ, or are you envious of the person who was an effective witness? When you hear about a major gift that is given to the church, are you envious of the one who gave the gift? When you hear that someone has more people attending his Bible study than you have attending the one in your home, do you rejoice that people are studying the Bible, or are you envious that the "numbers" aren't in your favor?

Saul envied David for a third reason. His daughter seemed to love David more than she loved her daddy. In 1 Samuel 18:28–29, we read, "Thus Saul saw and knew that the LORD was with David, and that Michal, Saul's daughter, loved him; and Saul was still more afraid of David. So Saul became David's enemy continually." Have you felt envy when somebody else seemed to horn in on a friendship, or when the person you considered to be your best friend began spending time with another person? Have you ever found yourself competing for another person's affection, time, or recognition? That's envy. And it's ugly.

Jealousy vs. envy. I want to be clear: Jealousy and envy are two different things. To be jealous is to have a desire for something that is rightfully yours. The Bible says in many places that God is a *jealous* God. He is jealous for the affection, loyalty, praise, and worship of His people (Ex. 20:4–6; 34:12–15).

Jealousy is an emotional response that can work to our benefit. When we are jealous for the safety and well-being of our children, and out of our jealousy we limit the time they spend with unruly and ungodly children or we limit the time they spend watching TV programs and video games that are violent, our jealousy is taking a proper expression. When a wife joins her husband on an out-of-town business trip to safeguard him from any temptations he might encounter at the corporation's annual convention, jealousy is working for the benefit of the marriage and the family. There are times when we *need* to be more jealous and to safeguard more closely the things dear to us and that are rightfully ours.

To be consumed with jealousy, however, to the point of continual mistrust is unhealthy. It can destroy a relationship.

How does envy differ from jealousy? Envy is a desire to possess things, people, and honors that are *not* rightfully ours. It is wanting what rightfully belongs to someone else or what has rightfully been earned by someone else.

4. *Envy Is a Denial of the Goodness of God*

Many people live in denial. They have a false understanding of God's nature, and they deny the goodness of God at work.

What is your first response when you hear about a friend who has received an unexpected large inheritance from a distant relative? Is it a green-eyed response: "That should have happened to me instead of to him because I would have known better how to handle the money"? Or is your response an expression of joy: "Praise God! God certainly has been good to my friend"?

What is your first response when you hear about a coworker in your company who hasn't worked half as hard as you have worked, and yet this person suddenly lands an outstanding position with another company— definitely a promotion with a higher salary? Is it to say, "Wow, God has really blessed that person," or is it to moan, "He doesn't deserve that—good things like that never happen to *me*"?

What is your first response when your roommate rushes into your apartment and flashes a large diamond ring given to her by a handsome and godly man she has been dating for only three months—when you have been out on the dating circuit for years without finding Mr. Right? Do you say, "Praise God! How wonderful for her!" or do you say, "He would have been mine if I'd only been in the right place at the right time"?

Jesus told a story about a master who hired some day workers. He hired one at 6:00 A.M., one at 9:00 A.M., one at noon, another at 3:00 P.M., and one at 5:00 P.M. He said, "Work hard, and I will be back and pay all of you fair wages at the end of the day." Well, they worked and he returned. And he did something entirely countercultural. He paid everybody the same amount. It isn't hard to imagine the response. Those who had been hired early in the day began to murmur and grumble—both of which are often signs of envy. They said, "Hey, what's the deal? We worked a long time, and these fly-by-nights come in and work for an hour or so and you pay them the same wages?" They were blessed, but they couldn't stand the fact that others had been equally blessed.

The Lord delights in giving good gifts to His people. He rewards those who diligently seek Him (Heb. 11:6). God gives to people out of the abundant goodness of His loving heart. Who are we to say that the God who is just in all things is being fair or unfair? God blesses, anoints, gifts, and endows people because *God chooses to do so for His purposes and for the fulfillment of His plan for us as individuals and as the body of Christ.*

There is never any justification for envy. And there is never any beauty in envy. It is an ugly, ugly sin.

FOUR FABULOUS THINGS YOU CAN DO TO RID YOURSELF OF ENVY

1. Call Envy What It Is

Come clean with yourself and with God. Own up to the envy you have harbored in your heart. Quit lying to yourself and to God about the envy you feel in your heart that motivates you to use alibis, smoke screens, plastic praise, mean motives, and condescending compliments.

What are you fixated on? Do you want someone else's spouse, someone else's personality, someone else's portfolio, someone else's office, someone else's [you fill in the blank]? That's envy. Call it what it is.

James urged, "Confess your trespasses to one another, and pray for one another, that you may be healed" (5:16). Recently my wife, Lisa, and I had dinner with another couple, and we began to talk about envy. Each of us admitted a struggle with envy—in other words, we "confessed" the envy we had felt from time to time. Later, Lisa and I admitted to each other how much freer we felt in our hearts after that time of confession. Owning up to your envy and admitting it not only to yourself but to someone who loves you can be a liberating experience.

It is even more liberating to confess to God the envy you feel. God already knows what is in your heart, but then you can know that you have "come clean" before God.

When you confess your envy, ask God to forgive you and to help you so that envy will not creep back into your soul.

2. Develop an Attitude of Gratitude

Do you have an attitude of gratitude? Romans 12:15 asserts, "Rejoice with those who rejoice, and weep with those who weep." The person with an envious attitude usually reverses the verse. The envious person rejoices with those who weep, and weeps with those who rejoice.

Choose to be genuinely pleased and excited when good things happen to others. When another person's child is part of a softball team that beats your child's team 15–0, clasp the hand of that child's father and say, "Hey, way to go. Your kid did great. What a team!" When a fellow salesperson walks away with the Salesman of the Year award, beating you by only the narrowest margin, warmly congratulate him. When the person who is vying for the same job you are seeking gets the job, write a note to that person: "I sincerely hope that you succeed and that many good things come to you in your new position."

Don't be a sore loser. Don't be concerned about what other people are gaining, thinking only about what you might be losing. Thank God for their success and trust God to provide for you *exactly* what you need to fill you and fulfill you.

I recently heard about a man who had been fired from a media-related job he had held for nearly fifteen years. His employer had not merely fired him, but had done so in a way that left the man feeling embarrassed in front of his peers. Another person on the staff was promoted immediately to fill his position. Rather than become bitter, this man wrote a letter of encouragement to the man who replaced him. He forgave his former employer and asked God to forgive him for his anger and his envy. He then wrote a kind letter to his former employer, thanking him for the many years of experience and the skills he had gained while working there.

In the course of the next few months, this man sent out dozens of résumés. He also took some aptitude testing and got career counseling. The more he began to look to the future with hope, the more he realized that he had a desire to pursue a different line of work.

This man was an ordained minister, although he had been engaged in ministry only on a part-time basis. One day as he was reading through the want ads, he came across an ad for a chaplaincy position at a private school for troubled teenage boys. He applied for the job and was hired.

Where did an attitude of gratitude fit into this story? When the person responsible for hiring him called to get references, whom did he call? First, he called the person who had been hired to replace this man. That person had the highest praise for him, not only as an employee, but as a person able to give encouragement "even in difficult times." The next person he called was the man's former employer, who also gave him a good recommendation and cited specifically that he had always been a man of high integrity and good character.

Did gratefulness play a role here? I believe it did. And even if neither man from his former place of employment had spoken well of him, *God* knew the state of his heart.

Don't be so concerned about what others have to the point that you forget to be thankful for what you have. I often encounter people who are envious of others' homes. I know the cure for that envy: Work in a homeless shelter for a while, or go on a two-week mission to an area that has been hit hard by a hurricane, flood, tornado, or other natural disaster. Be grateful for what you have.

Other people I know are envious of the appearance or the physique of another person. They say, "I wish I had that body! Then I'd be somebody!" What is the cure for that envy? Volunteer for six months in a hospital that helps with the rehabilitation of paraplegics or those who have been badly burned.

Thank God for every good thing in your life. Appreciate what He has given you, is giving you, and will give you. Remember that "every good gift and every perfect gift is from above, and comes down from the Father of lights" (James 1:17).

3. Expect Envy

No one is entirely immune from envy, just as no one can ever fully avoid pride or anger. Anticipate that you will have to confront this green-eyed monster of envy at some point in your life.

I have discovered that I tend to feel more envy when certain times of the year roll around, when I am with certain people, when I drive through certain neighborhoods, and when I walk through certain malls. Something goes off inside me, sending the message, "You deserve *that*, Ed, just as much or more than the person who has it. You've got to have *that*, Ed. You are just as good as the person who lives there or owns that." I have learned what triggers an envious spirit in me.

What is the cure? I increase my praise and thanksgiving to God during those times of year when I seem to be more envy-prone. I avoid being around people who are always talking about what they have or what they have earned. If I cannot avoid being with them, I make an effort to rejoice with them over the good things they are experiencing.

I stay out of certain neighborhoods, and if I must travel through them, I make it a point to pray for the people who live in the houses I pass.

I stay out of certain malls as much as possible, and when I do shop there, I thank the Lord that He has enabled people to design, create, or manufacture so many wonderful things.

If I cannot avoid a situation that triggers envy in me,

I make an effort to find a way to praise and thank God in the midst of it. Identify what triggers *your* envy, and then make a game plan for dealing with those things.

4. *Practice Pursuing God*

In 1 Peter 2:1–2, Peter wrote, "Laying aside all . . . envy . . . as newborn babes, desire the pure milk of the word, that you may grow thereby." In Galatians 5:25–26, Paul wrote, "If we live in the Spirit, let us also walk in the Spirit. Let us not become conceited, provoking one another, envying one another." Peter and Paul spoke to the same point: The best way to defeat envy in your life is to pursue God rather than things.

God is not an extracurricular activity. God says to you, "Pursue Me." He wants to be the object of your desire, your central thought, your top priority. When you pursue God and focus on Him, other stuff doesn't matter nearly as much. It loses its luster.

Getting involved in God's stuff—God's agenda, God's purpose for your life, God's concerns—keeps you from getting involved in other people's stuff.

MOVE FROM A SCOWL TO A SMILE

The person who is not envious is a person who replaces the scowl of envy with a genuine smile at the success of others.

The person who is not envious is a person who replaces the squinty eyes of scrutiny and disdain with a wide-eyed appreciation for all of the good things that God gives.

The person who is not envious is a person without big ol' teeth that seek to devour what another person has, and without big ol' ears that are just waiting for the gossip that will destroy another person's reputation.

The person who is thankful is a person who is a pleasure to be around, and a person who attracts the friendship of others.

The decision to be envious and anxious, or thankful and content, is a choice you make with your free will. Choose today to slay the ugly green-eyed monster called envy!

5

SLOTHFULNESS

Getting in Gear About the Right Things

The sloth is a lazy, lumbering creature that hangs by its claws for days at a time. It's an animal the crocodile would laugh at because it does absolutely nothing.

For the most part they eat, sleep, and occasionally mate. If threatened, they emit a low, plaintive cry, but this hardly ever happens since they seldom come to the ground and rarely are in danger.

Most people I know have more in common with this creature than they care to admit. In the animal kingdom, this spiritless animal might be regarded as docile. In the human kingdom, those who are slothful face a much different fate. Slothfulness is one of the seven deadly sins.

In the first chapter of this book, we discussed sins of omission. Slothfulness is perhaps the foremost sin of omission. Slothful people do nothing, and in doing nothing, they omit many good things they could have done.

Do We Really Have to Deal with Sloth Today?

Many believe that the first theologians to compile the original list of seven deadly sins put sloth at the top of the list. When I first read that, I figured that a lot of people in the Middle Ages must have been lazy. After all, a knight only had to rescue a fair maiden from the clutches of a fire-breathing dragon now and then. While awaiting these rare moments of valor, he would no doubt polish his armor, eat chicken and throw the bones on the castle floor. I said to myself, *We don't deal with sloth. We're a culture that has developed a colossal collection of workaholics. Psychologists are continually telling us to chill out, slow down, and smell the roses.*

If I ask any particular group of people if they are slothful, I rarely get any takers. The response is usually, "No way, Ed. I'm so busy, I don't know if I'm coming or going." We are a nation of people dedicated to working strategically, playing competitively, and keeping house immaculately.

The truth is that every generation has been just as busy with work as any other generation. There have always been the idle rich and the idle poor, sick, and feeble, but the vast majority of people have worked from dawn to dusk—they have just worked at different jobs and have had different priorities.

The fact is, sloth has very little to do with work or even the pace of life. It has to do with whether we are lazy about the important things of life. Sloth is selective. It is moving slowly when we should be moving speedily and purposefully. It is hanging around when we should be taking on a challenge. And most of us must admit that we are slothful in certain areas of our lives, and most of the time, these are also the most important areas of life.

THE SEDUCTIVE SIDES OF SLOTH

Sloth has a number of seductive qualities to it. It lulls us into complacency, apathy, and inactivity. I want to show you several seductive sides of sloth described in Mark's gospel.

Sloth Can Make Us Too Lethargic to Love

We have a very clear example in one of the most dramatic moments of the Bible. Jesus was facing His final hours on this earth. He knew He was about to be betrayed, arrested, tried in a kangaroo court, and crucified on a Roman cross. To prepare Himself for what He knew was ahead—the sacrifice of His life for the sins of the world—He went to a garden to pray. I've been to the Garden of Gethsemane, and it is a beautiful, private garden—a great retreat spot. Jesus took Peter, James, and John with Him, and He said to the three trusted disciples, "My soul is exceedingly sorrowful, even to death. Stay here and watch" (Mark 14:34).

Jesus was trusting the deeply committed disciples to help Him—to support Him with their presence, to pray with Him, to minister to Him, to demonstrate their love for Him. Of all people on earth, surely Peter, James, and John would help Jesus in His time of need.

What happened? Jesus went a little farther into the garden and began to pray, and when He returned to where He had left Peter, James, and John, He found them asleep! Jesus said to Peter, "Simon, are you sleeping? Could you not watch one hour?" (Mark 14:37).

Can you hear both the compassion and the hurt in Jesus' voice? Many of us would likely be so embarrassed and so convicted at hearing Jesus speak to us in that way that we would be *determined* to stay awake and pray from that moment on. Or would we?

Let's apply this to where you live. Picture yourself coming home after a hard day of work. You are tired. You have had a tough time on the job. You realize that behind your front door await your wife and your children and a whole bunch of opportunities to express love for them. You have the opportunity to engage your bride in meaningful conversation and to express appreciation to her.

You have the opportunity to play with your children, help them with their homework, read a story to them, and pray with them as you tuck them into bed. But on this particular evening, you are tired. You have the daily paper in one hand and a video in the other, and you intend to "veg"—to sit in your favorite chair, watch a little ESPN, and pop in the video. If you're lucky, you'll be too busy snoring to see the end of the movie.

The opportunities to express love go out the window. Not because you are a mean person. Not because you are cruel. Not because you intentionally want to harm your wife and children. But because you are slothful. You haven't chosen to do what is the most important, needful, and right thing to do. You have been too lethargic to love.

Many of us have problems in relationships primarily because we are lazy. We are too lazy to express kindness, to take the time for genuine conversation, or to spend time with a person who needs us.

Lots of people are fired-up workers. They hit the marketplace, and they're churning, they're shaking, they're baking, and they're raking in the cash. They go home, though, and what do their spouses and children get? Leftovers. That's slothfulness.

Is your marriage in need of a little romantic spice and creativity? Do you recognize that things have gone a little stale, and yet you fail to do anything about it? You might say, "Love just flows. If you have to work at it, it isn't love." Nothing could be farther from the truth. Love is a verb—an *action* verb. It is expressed in the *doing* of things that are pleasant, meaningful, and appreciated by the person you love. Are you willing to make the effort to do what you know your spouse needs? Love takes work, intentional decisions, commitment, and time.

A man said to me, "I'm just not in love with my wife anymore. I don't feel any love for her."

I replied, "When was the last time you did something loving toward her?" Love isn't a feeling. It's a commitment. It's not that we feel love and then we express it. We must express love, and then we feel it.

Is your relationship with your children all that it could be? Do you recognize that your children need more of your time and attention, and yet you fail to adjust your priorities to give them what they need? A parent might say, "When things calm down a little at work, I'll make more time for my children." The problem is, things rarely calm down at work. Children need a parent's affection, attention, and time all through their growing-up years—every day, every month, every year.

Is it too much of a bother to offer a coworker a ride home from work when you know that this coworker is having car trouble? Is it too much of a bother to offer to baby-sit the children so your spouse can have a night out with friends? Is it too much of a bother to take the trash out without being asked, to stop and pick up the dry cleaning on the way home to save your spouse an extra trip, to put your socks in the laundry basket rather than throw them on the floor? Is it too much of a nuisance to remember a birthday or an anniversary?

Sloth takes many subtle forms, but perhaps the most deadly form is being too lethargic to love.

Sloth Can Make Us Too Sluggish to Stand

Jesus said to Peter, "Watch and pray." The tense of these words in the Greek language really means, "Watch and keep on watching, and pray and keep on praying." Jesus told Peter to remain in a state of watching and praying. Why? Jesus said, "Lest you enter into temptation" (Mark 14:37–38).

Jesus knew a lot about temptation. His first assignment after His baptism was to go one-on-one with Satan. Jesus was in the wilderness fasting and praying for forty days and nights. Every time Jesus' body said, "Feed Me," Jesus said no. When the evil one went after Jesus, tempting Him to depart from His life's mission—which is always what Satan will tempt a person to do—Jesus said no. Jesus had been saying no to food for so many days, it was just one more step to say no to Satan.

By the time Jesus encountered Satan face-to-face, He had been saying no to self and yes to God's will for more than three decades. He had a life habit of saying no to evil.

Sloth lulls us into saying yes to our basic impulse to do nothing. It lulls us into saying yes only to what feels good and feels easy.

If we say yes to every dessert that comes along, to every

flirtatious invitation, to every exaggerated sales pitch, to every opportunity to pad our expense account, what makes us think we are going to say no when Satan throws his best punches?

Long after Peter had fallen asleep in the Garden of Gethsemane, long after he had denied knowing Jesus three times, and long after Jesus had forgiven Peter and restored him to ministry, Peter wrote these words: "Be sober, be vigilant; because your adversary the devil walks about like a roaring lion, seeking whom he may devour. Resist him, steadfast in the faith" (1 Peter 5:8–9). Peter knew what he was talking about.

Some time ago, my wife brought home a little gray cat for our children. I'm not a great cat lover, but I have to admit, this little cat stole my heart. Ranger was a sweet cat that loved to be around people. A lot of cats have an attitude of "Forget you," but Ranger would lumber out to my car to greet me at the end of a day just like a dog. One day when I went out to my car to go to work, I found our little cat ripped apart and lying dead in the driveway.

Ranger hadn't been alert. He hadn't paid enough attention. He had been attacked by a coyote.

Resistance is active. Vigilance is active. Steadfastness is active. Slothfulness is not. It is the very opposite. Slothfulness is rolling over and giving in. Slothfulness is closing one's eyes to the world. Slothfulness is yielding to every little temptation that comes along. Slothfulness is refusing to pay attention at all times to what is important.

Slothful supplications. People often pray what I call prayers of slothful supplication about problems in their lives. They pray one time and think they've dealt with the issue. For example, they pray, "God, right now I pray that You will deliver me from the desire to overeat." They assume that God will give them a great desire for tofu and salads for the rest of their lives, and they will never want a candy bar again. That's sloppy and slothful supplication.

Or people pray, "God, right now, deliver me from my hot temper!" Or they pray, "Okay, God, deliver me from these sexually impure thoughts." They expect an instant lifetime personality overhaul. But is that the way God works? No.

We must daily take our stand for righteousness against evil, wrong attitudes, and bad behaviors. It's a continual thing. We must die to self and ask God for the strength and power to stand. We must actively resist the temptation to become sluggish.

Sloth Can Make Us Too Mellow to Move

Jesus told His disciples, "The spirit is willing, but the body is weak" (Mark 14:38 NIV). The older we get, the more we can relate to what He said! Few of us, however, want to pay the price of discipline.

Do you want to be a smashing tennis player? A person can say he wants to be a better player every day for months and never improve his tennis game. Effort is required—the discipline to get out there, play the game, and practice ground strokes and serves by the hour.

Do you want to get in better shape? Nothing will happen until you start to run laps and lift weights, or do some other kind of regular physical activity.

Do you want to grow your company? Nothing happens unless you exert effort and practice hard work.

We have a built-in inertia to keep from moving—to lie low and bide our time, to sit back and watch, to relax and enjoy. We'd rather *think* about playing tennis, take a quick pill to lose weight, or dream about financial success than *do* what is required.

You might be saying, "Well, Ed, I'm just a laid-back person." Having a mellow personality is fine. But too often being laid-back means lying back and letting others make the effort. Slothfulness has nothing to do with personality. It has to do with whether we will expend the effort required to do what God wants us to do.

A second time Jesus went away to pray, and again, He returned and found His top three disciples asleep. He said, "Are you still sleeping and resting? It is enough! The hour has come; behold, the Son of Man is being betrayed into the hands of sinners" (Mark 14:41). Eventually the hour for action passes, and we lose our opportunity. With lost opportunity comes lost meaning for our lives.

The disciples had a chance to minister to Jesus, to help Him, to strengthen Him—but they missed it. They were asleep in sloth.

Sloth is someplace between slime and sludge, neither of which moves very fast, and both of which are undesirable.

No Slack Is Cut for Sloth

Jesus had a great deal to say about slothfulness. One day He drove the lane and slam-dunked a message about sloth. He told three stories aimed directly at this fatal distraction. They are found in Matthew 25.

No Excuse for Failing to Prepare

In the first story Jesus described a group of bridesmaids who were waiting for a bridal parade.

In Jewish culture, the bridegroom would go to the bride's house to pick up his bride, and there would be a parade back to the groom's house for a big ceremony and a banquet that would often last an entire week. Jesus' illustration was about ten bridesmaids who were waiting to join the parade. Five of them were wise, and they brought lamps with them and oil for the lamps. The other five were airheads who brought lamps but no oil.

The parade began about midnight, and the ones who had oil in their lamps joined the parade. They made it all the way to the groom's house and enjoyed the party. The bridesmaids who were looking at their nails and worrying about their hair and forgot their oil began to search frantically. They finally found some oil and ran to the party and tried to enter, but the groom said there was no room for them. They were stranded on the street because of *sloth* (Matt. 25:1–13).

Four things were required of these bridesmaids—four things they failed to do. These same things are required of us:

1. We have a responsibility for *knowing* what God desires for us to do with our lives.

2. We have a responsibility for *planning* for our eternal future.

3. We have a responsibility for *zeroing in* on what is most important.

4. We have a responsibility for *being sensitive* to God's timing.

There's no good excuse for becoming stranded in sloth.

No Excuse for Failing to Try

Jesus also told a story about a wealthy entrepreneur who was getting ready to take an exotic trip. He met with three of his workers and gave the first worker five thousand dollars, the second worker two thousand dollars, and the third worker one thousand dollars. Then he left.

The entrepreneur was gone for a long time, but one day he returned and said, "Show me the money." The one who had been given five thousand dollars showed his portfolio, and he gave the master back ten thousand dollars. The boss gave him a high five and said, "Well done!" The one who was given two thousand dollars also doubled his money. Again the boss said, "Well done." The man who had been given one thousand dollars was next to report. What had he done? He had been stranded in sloth. He had dug a hole and buried the money in it. That news put the wealthy entrepreneur on tilt. He said, "Get out of here," and he pushed the slothful worker into darkness (Matt. 25:14–30).

Too many people give up and quit trying, saying to themselves, *What's the use? I'll never be as good as* _____. Or, they cut short their own accomplishments with the attitude, *I'm a loser. Other people win all the time and make big scores, but I'm just not in their league, so why try?*

God didn't call anybody to sit on the sidelines. He expects each person to be active. He expects each person to try— to give life his best shot with his faith, energy, and ability.

"But," you may be saying, "I'll never be able to double what I've been given. That's raising the bar too high."

How do you know you can't double the talents you've been given if you don't even try to develop them? How do you know you can't reach a high level of success if you don't make the effort to learn what you need to learn, practice what you know to practice, and do what you know to do?

You can't succeed at the interview if you don't show up for it. You won't get the job unless you apply for it. And who knows how far you might go, if you never take the first step in any direction?

Was it risky for the workers who were given five thousand dollars and two thousand dollars to invest that money? Yes. But it was even riskier for the man who didn't invest his money to bury it. He *knew* his master expected him to at least turn the money over to a banker so it could draw interest. He *knew* his master expected results.

It takes faith to overcome sloth. It also takes sustained effort over time, which requires discipline. And here's the point I don't want you to miss: Not only has the Lord given to each of us talents and abilities, but He has also given to every person a measure of faith and a free will. God has given us the power to make choices and to discipline our lives. Each one of us has been given these things to overcome slothfulness:

- *God-given ability*—aptitude for success in one or more areas of life and a capacity for intellectual development.

- *God-given life* and a degree of physical strength, energy, and flexibility.

- *God-given faith.* As Romans 12:3 tells us, "God has dealt to each one a measure of faith."

- *God-given will* with which to make choices and decisions, and to set priorities.

And God expects us to use what He has given us.

In this second parable, Jesus is telling each one of us, "There's no excuse for your slothfulness. It's not a matter of how much you have been given. It's a matter of what you do with what you have been given."

No Excuse for a Callous Heart

Jesus wasn't finished with His teaching about slothfulness after that second parable. He went on to give a third teaching that was even more direct. Jesus told a story about a king who judged his people according to whether they had done his will (Matt. 25:31–46).

To one group, the king said, "Get out of my sight. I was hungry, and you didn't feed me. I was thirsty, and you didn't hand me a glass of water, much less a Gatorade. I was a stranger, and you slammed the door in my face. I was naked, and you didn't even get me some clothes from Goodwill."

Those who were rejected said, "You're the king! When were *you* hungry or thirsty or naked or without a house?" And the king said, "You didn't do these things for the least of the subjects in my kingdom, and that means you didn't do them to me."

If you ask someone, "Why aren't you involved in a ministry of some type?" he will usually give you one of two answers:

I'm not a pastor. Ministry is not limited to those in full-time or part-time church jobs. Ministry is expected of every person who calls himself a Christian. To minister to another person is to help another person overcome the need in his life. If the need is practical and material, ministry must be practical and material. If the need is emotional or mental, ministry must be to the emotions or mind of the person. If the need is spiritual, ministry must address the spiritual well-being of the person. We are to do our best to meet needs wherever and whenever we find them.

Every person you meet has a need in some area of his life at any given time. You are to minister to that need to the best of your ability.

I don't know what the Lord would like for me to do as a ministry. I don't know how He wants me to be involved. My response to that is, "Look around." Open your eyes. Jesus was very practical in His teaching. He cited people who were obviously in need: hungry people, thirsty people, strangers, sick people, prisoners, and naked people. Those people still exist in our world today. We have shelters overflowing with homeless people, hospitals overflowing with patients, prisons overflowing with convicts, and thousands of people coming into our nation every year in search of work so they can feed and clothe their children.

We also meet people who have deep inner needs:

- A hunger to know God and to have more meaning in life;
- A thirst for the Word of God;

- A desire to be in fellowship with God and with other people;

- A desire to be healed of some emotional weakness, injury, or sickness;

- A desire to be free of bad memories, bad dreams, harmful addictions, and gripping fear; and

- A desire to be clothed with a new identity—one that is strong, whole, and pure before God.

The problem is not that we are unaware of the needs all around us—the problem is that we don't want to do anything about the needs. We want to shut our eyes and hope they will go away. We don't want to face our own problems, much less take on the problems of others. It's a matter of *slothfulness*.

Your response to all this may be, "But there's so much to do. What could I possibly do that would make any difference?"

Look again at what Jesus said. He doesn't expect you to personally conquer all of the needs of every person on the planet. He said, "When you see a hungry person, give him a meal." He didn't say you were to adopt him, take him home, and feed him three squares a day for the rest of his life. He rewarded those who gave a cup of water to the thirsty, shelter for a while to the stranger, a set of clothing to the naked person. He rewarded those who visited the sick and those in prison.

The Lord doesn't ask us to do anything that we are incapable of doing. But He does command us to do *something*.

How do you respond to the person who comes to work with eyes swollen from a night of crying? Do you ignore that person, thinking it is more polite to look the other way? Is that what Jesus would do?

How do you respond to the person who lives in the neighborhood next to yours and has his home destroyed by a fire? Do you shrug your shoulders and expect the local relief agency and the insurance company to provide for his needs?

How do you respond to the person in your Sunday school class who is going through a divorce? Do you avoid her because you don't know what to say?

How do you respond to the person in your church who is ill with cancer? Do you call on that person, or do you stay away because you don't want to bother the family or get in the way?

Slothfulness.

That ol' sloth just keeps sleepin', swingin' from the tree, hopin' that things will be all right when he wakes up.

WHERE ARE YOU SPIRITUALLY SLOTHFUL?

In what area of your life are you spiritually slothful? Psychologist and author M. Scott Peck has said, "Laziness is the single greatest impediment to spiritual growth." As a pastor, I agree!

There are five stages in spiritual growth, and each stage is an area in which we must not let slothfulness keep us from doing what the Lord desires for us to do. I call these stages the five S's.

1. *Salvation*

When Paul was in prison, he had a chance to meet Felix. Felix called a meeting with Paul in order to decide his fate, and Paul ended up preaching a sermon to him about the Christian life. The Bible says the ungodly ruler heard the message and his heart began to beat fast. But here is what he said to Paul: "Paul, I hear you and I believe you, but I'll call for you to speak to me again at a more convenient time. I'll get my life right at a more convenient moment." That convenient moment never came again for Felix.

Why don't you settle the issue of eternity today? Why don't you make *now* the time you get to know Christ personally?

Some people sit on information about their personal salvation for a great length of time. They know that all they need to do is to make a faith decision to confess their sins to God, receive His forgiveness, and be cleansed of their sins. But they sit back and fail to make that move.

Don't let slothfulness keep you from Christ Jesus. Don't let slothfulness keep you from receiving God's forgiveness and from knowing that you are eternally in relationship with God your Creator. The Bible announces, "Now is the day of salvation" (2 Cor. 6:2 NIV). Don't delay!

Other people know they have accepted Christ, but they have never taken the step of water baptism. They are just one pastoral conversation, one baptismal service away from being baptized. Each time they attend a baptismal service they say, "Well, maybe next time." Make this time the last time you say "next time"! Don't give in to slothfulness.

2. Small Groups

We have a large church, and the best way in which people can truly become involved with one another on a Monday-through-Saturday basis is to become part of a small group. This is true for the church as a whole. None of us are likely to be involved with every person in the church we attend. We must build relationships within the larger body.

This certainly doesn't mean developing exclusive clique groups. It does mean taking advantage of every opportunity to get together with other believers and to enter into a giving and receiving relationship with them. The Bible teaches, "Let us consider one another in order to stir up love and good works, not forsaking the assembling of ourselves together" (Heb. 10:24–25).

We have two types of small groups in our church—groups organized around Bible study that meet at the church building, and groups called Home Teams that meet throughout the greater geographic area served by our church. Both types have been developed for people of various ages, including groups for singles, married couples without children, married couples with young children, and so forth. Most churches offer similar opportunities, perhaps not in exactly the same way we do, but opportunities, nevertheless, for people to get better acquainted with those who sit in the same building with them on Sunday morning.

Becoming involved with a small group of believers requires action. Friendship doesn't happen automatically. It requires time, attention, and effort.

Overcome your fear of vulnerability, adjust your schedule, face your reluctance to become involved with others, and refuse to give in to slothfulness. Once you get involved, you'll wonder how you made it without a small group.

3. Spiritual Gifts

The Bible teaches us that we all have unique spiritual abilities and that these abilities are to be used to build up our local churches.

The development of your spiritual gifts requires action on your part. The person who is gifted in teaching, for example, needs to develop that gift and become the best teacher possible. The person who is gifted to be a good administrator must find an outlet for using that gift of administration. The same is true for a person with a gift of hospitality or a gift of service.

We learn best by doing. We grow through experience.

We become better at any gift we have been given by God through practice.

4. *Seed Sowing*

Are you aware that the Bible has more to say about giving than about any other subject? So often people say, "All the church wants is my money." That's an excuse people often use for *not* giving. As Dave Ramsey says, "All the credit card companies want is your money. The *church* actually does care about people."

The Bible teaches us that we are to be seed sowers. We are to plant our giving in the best soil possible and to look to God to produce an abundant harvest for our benefit. The biblical standard is 10 percent of a person's income given to the work of the Lord. People ask me if they should tithe on gross income or net income. I ask them whether they want God to bless the gross or the net. It's their choice.

What is the benefit to the person doing the giving?

Jesus taught, "Give, and it will be given to you: good measure, pressed down, shaken together, and running over will be put into your bosom. For with the same measure that you use, it will be measured back to you" (Luke 6:38).

God wants His people to be cheerful, generous givers. Giving opens us up. It becomes an attitude, not just an act. Giving extends to all our resources, not just our money. It includes our time, our energy, our creativity.

One last thing about giving. Giving requires intention

and effort. Money doesn't just hop into the offering plate without our putting it there. Budgets just don't automatically produce a 10 percent gift to God's work. Responding to a particular need with a special offering requires spiritual eyes to see the need and a generous heart.

Don't let slothfulness keep you from giving and from receiving a blessing from God.

5. *Sharing Your Faith with Others*

We are called to be witnesses of the love of Jesus Christ. We are called to be ambassadors for the faith—sharing the gospel with every person we meet to the extent he is willing to listen to us. God doesn't call us to take our Bibles and hit others over the head with them, saying, "If you don't turn, you'll burn." He does call us to speak the name of Jesus, to give godly counsel, to express godly opinions, to live pure lives that others can observe, and to love those who are hell-bound.

When opportunity arises, we are to tell others what Jesus has done for us personally. We don't need to be theologians or Bible experts—witnesses are called to the stand of justice solely to tell what they personally saw, heard, and experienced. That's our role in telling others about Jesus Christ.

Do you invite people to church? Do you make an effort to get people into closer proximity to the Lord and into a place where they can hear the gospel preached and see the love of God in action?

Stop worrying about your reputation. Stop worrying about whether the person will receive Christ. Stop worrying about whether you are making a mistake in the way you witness. Your job is not to save a person's soul, but to bring a person to a place where he can encounter Jesus Christ.

Don't be slothful in your witness for Christ!

HOW DO YOU GET RID OF SLOTH?

Seek God's Forgiveness

Face the fact that you have been slothful, and ask the Lord to forgive you. Ask Him to forgive you for all of the opportunities you've missed, all of the roads you should have taken but didn't, and all of the decisions and actions you should have made and taken but didn't.

Open Your Eyes

Ask the Lord to open your eyes to *His* opportunities. Ask Him to help you see the world as He sees it. Ask Him to help you grow in the areas where you need to grow. The worst kind of slothfulness is failing to address deadly hang-ups and saying, "I'll take care of that sin later, not now." Open your eyes!

Set a Goal

Pick an area for growth. Focus on one thing to do first. Don't try to change every area of your life at once.

Zero in on one particular area and one particular step in that area. Set an achievable goal.

Buddy Up with a Friend

Invite a friend to join you in your quest to overcome slothfulness. Ideally that friend should be fighting the same battle you are fighting. For example, if you feel a need to start walking to get fit, find a walking partner. If you feel a need to get involved in a Bible study, find a friend who will go with you to a Bible study group.

Ask for God's Help

Ask God to help you each time you engage in the activity you know you should be doing. For example, if your goal is to walk every morning, when you wake up, ask the Lord to help you get out of bed and put on your walking shoes. Or if your goal is to curb your spending, know and plan what you want to purchase before you leave the house, and then ask the Lord to help you every time you walk into a store.

Thank God

Thank the Lord for each opportunity He sends your way to grow in His grace and to practice the spiritual gifts He has given you. Thank Him for being faithful to you, even in times when you haven't been faithful to Him.

MOTIVATION IS YOUR RESPONSIBILITY

Ultimately motivation is *your* responsibility. Other people may inspire you and help motivate you, but there's no substitute for self-motivation. It's the only motivation that lasts over time.

Choose to get in gear—about the right things, the important things, the things that are truly pleasing to God.

Choose to smash sloth out of your life.

LUST

Putting the Big Chill on Undesirable Desires

I t has always been my dream to host my own fishing show. That may seem like a strange thing for a pastor to say, but I love to fish. I enjoy watching fishing programs, and through the years, I have daydreamed about what it would be like to have a fishing program of my own. A while back, a member of our church gave me that opportunity. I called the little program *The Pastor Caster*, and the topic was bass fishing. Well, sorta.

I went out to a little lake with Dennis Brewer, a friend of mine, in search of "the big one"—which in fishing talk is usually the one fish in every lake that nobody has ever caught and few have ever seen. This particular lake was known for producing, on occasion, trophy bass. The day we did our little program, no such fish emerged. So, I turned the fishing program into an illustrated sermon, and I pointed out to my church these two key facts about what it takes to land giant bass:

1. *All obstacles must be overcome—regardless.* Every time a person goes out to fish, he has to overcome a few obstacles. An obstacle we encountered that day was a very large NO TRESPASSING sign. We concluded, "That couldn't possibly mean us." To the warning, AREA PATROLLED, we said, "No big deal." To the warning that read, PROSECUTORS WILL BE VIOLATED TO THE FULLEST EXTENT OF THE LAW, we said, "They'll have to catch us first. And after all, I'm fishing with our church attorney!"

We had permission to use the lake where we were fishing, but the truth is, most of us approach life with an all-obstacles-must-be overcome mind-set. We are good at getting past all the warning signs without any loss of speed.

2. *The finest equipment must be used.* When you go in search of giant bass, you need to have the best equipment. Our particular fishing boat was made of high-quality, extremely sturdy, only slightly chipped fiberglass. We used a jig that was very fancy, with a feathered skirt on it to attract the fish, and on the back of the hook, we put a piece of Uncle Josh pork rind to spice things up.

In life, most of us think we've got what it takes to get all we want.

Armed with this twofold advice, we went fishing. The

experience was humorous for the congregation to watch. But the music underscore packed a punch with the message: "Those fish have got me hooked."

I added my own theme song, "You get a line and I'll get a pole, babe. Yeah—you get a line and I'll get a pole, and we'll take you down to the old trophy bass hole—honey, baby, mine."

The video was a perfect setup for talking about another kind of fishing and another kind of lure. Every day, in countless and sometimes unbelievable ways, we face the lure of lust. The bait is always dangling in front of us. We're "trophy fish" that the devil is hoping to catch.

A Temptation That Touches Every Person

James 1:14 warns, "But each one is tempted when he is drawn away by his own desires and enticed." I looked up the word *enticed* in the Greek language, and I discovered that the word is actually a fishing term. It means to lure by using bait. And James said that nobody is exempt.

Lust probably has more gender differences than any of the other fatal distractions. Women seem to have a number of definitions for lust. For men, the term is rather straightforward—it refers to sexual desire. Lust can be subtle to women. It is rarely subtle for men.

When they encounter the word *lust,* many people feel a

stab like a knife in their hearts. They know they have fallen prey to lust in the past. They may be participating in it in the present. They fear they may fall for the trap again. Nearly everybody knows what it feels like to lust after someone or something. Nearly everybody has given in to the temptation of lust, if not in reality, at least in his imagination.

Lust looms large in our world. It's "in." We use it to sell things and as an excuse to buy things. We read about it and endorse it.

Lust is casting a lingering look at the newly hired secretary. It is deciding to conduct business at a local men's club. It is surfing the Internet for yet another image to download into a private file. It is a group of guys huddling around a magazine rack, gawking at the latest *Playboy* centerfold or the swimsuit edition of *Sports Illustrated*.

Lust plays on our sexuality, but it does not satisfy us sexually.

FOUR TRICKS OF THE OL' ANGLER

Satan is a highly competent fisherman. He has been angling for human souls for years, and one of his prime jigs is lust. He knows that more Christians fall victim to sexual lust than just about any other type of sin. Let me share with you four things that the Ol' Angler does when he goes out on the lake to catch us.

1. Choosing the Best Time and Place

Satan takes his handy rod and reel, he stands in his boat, he checks out his spiritual depth finder, and he determines the best place on the lake for the fish he wants to catch. He is acutely aware of the type of fish he wants to catch, the place to find those fish, and the time of day when the fish are most likely to bite.

How many times have you seen an angler standing out in the middle of a river with his rod and reel instead of at the water's edge? How many times have you seen a bass fishing boat turn suddenly into one particular inlet on the lake? Serious fishermen are always in search of just the right place to cast. Satan follows the same approach. He goes to the places where people usually go when they are most tired, most bored, and most off guard to his temptation.

The skilled angler also knows the best time of day—and the best times of the month or year—to go fishing. Satan is an expert at reading your particular "seasons." He knows the times when your energy is low, your morale is low, you feel a little depressed, or your spiritual disciplines have been lacking. These are the times he goes fishing for you.

The Ol' Angler also looks at the spiritual depth finder of your life. He sees where you are vulnerable, which is often where you feel invincible. He knows how "deep" your commitment is.

2. *Choosing the Best Lure*

After the fisherman is at the right fishing hole, he must determine the best lure for catching the type of fish he wants. A jig is the number one lure for catching trophy bass. The best jig is one with a little skirt on it to hide the hook. What a great illustration that is for the lure of sexual lust! Satan always tempts us with an appearance that looks innocent and intriguing. He never reveals the deadly hook.

Having the right lure is not enough, of course. The fisherman must know how to use the lure. The expert fisherman knows that when a jig is cast out on the water, it must be presented to the fish as discreetly as possible. No plopping sounds. No talking. No giving away the intent of the fisherman. The skilled angler seeks to drop the jig onto the surface of the water as gently as possible, as if it is a live insect.

Satan's best lures for human beings seem to follow the same tactic. He presents something that is pleasant to the eye. No big fanfare. No glaring lights or blaring trumpets to announce the arrival of the temptation. Just a quiet encounter—an opportunity. His temptations begin with a glance, a soft touch, a slight movement, a wink, a smile.

No sin is involved in the casting of a lure or the presence of a lure in the water. Some Christians seem to think they have sinned if they are tempted. The truth is, all people are tempted, no matter how spiritually mature they are. Satan continues to cast his lures throughout a person's life, regardless of his age, his ministry, or his outstanding reputation.

3. *Working the Lure*

Once the lure has been cast onto the water, the expert fisherman begins to work the line. He allows the lure to sink to a certain depth, and then he slowly reels in the line.

Satan follows the same technique. He works the temptation. He isn't in a hurry. He has been doing this for thousands of years, and he has become very skilled at the "slow tempt."

The temptation may be eye contact that is a little different from before.

Or the joke that has a lustful overtone.

Or the lingering business lunch with a member of the opposite sex.

The question arises, "What would it be like . . . ?" The imagination kicks in, and the fish begins to draw closer to the bait—not yet striking at it, but aware of it and moving toward it.

Anytime a person begins to dwell in his mind on the possibility of sin, he is on his way toward sinning. That's why it is so important to stop temptation at this point.

Let's be very clear: Lust is not seeing a beautiful woman or a handsome man and thinking, *That's a beautiful woman,* or *That guy's a hunk.* I like what Billy Graham said about lust: "The first look does not get us in trouble." It's the second look. It's the third look. Lust takes over when you start to picture yourself with this person sexually.

You can't keep Satan from tempting you. You can't keep him from enticing your curiosity or engaging your imagination. But you can put a stop to the temptation at precisely that point. You can say, "I will *not* think about that. I will *not* entertain that question. I will *not* allow my imagination to go in that direction."

Proverbs 23:7 tells us, "As he thinks in his heart, so is he." Jesus called men to be aware of the lust that causes a man to commit adultery "in his heart" (Matt. 5:27–28).

4. *Embedding the Hook*

Satan's goal is to get a person to engage in an act of sin—to "take the bait."

When a bass strikes at a lure and swallows it, that bass has no idea whatsoever that it has just swallowed a hook. It strikes the lure and swims away happily with no thought of danger.

That's also what happens when most people take the bait of lust. They engage in an act of lustful sin, and they go on about their lives without any thought that they may have just set in motion a string of terrible and even deadly consequences.

Those who engage in premarital sex thinking that they were "just having sex" rarely see their behavior as "trying to make a baby." Those who "experiment" with adultery seldom think they are setting the time bomb for the destruction of their marriage. Most people who commit sexual sin are in serious denial about their sin. They believe that they will never get caught and that somehow, life will continue to move toward a happily-ever-after ending.

When the fisherman tightens the line, the hook is embedded in the jaw of the fish, and things take on a whole new dimension! The same goes for sexual sin. A person can go only so long before he reaches the end of the line and the hook is set.

The wife—or husband—finds out.

The pregnancy test strip is an undesirable color.

Rejection takes the form of being fired from a job.

The diagnosis is herpes.

The mistress—or lover—begins to make blackmail demands.

The HIV test comes back positive.

The hook is set. And the pain begins.

An old proverb declares, "Your sin will find you out." The Bible version is this: "Who [The Lord] will both bring to light the hidden things of darkness and reveal the counsels of the hearts" (1 Cor. 4:5). Even if you go your entire life without your sin coming to light, it eventually will be revealed.

The fight. Once a bass feels that embedded hook, it begins to fight. It splashes and thrashes. In most cases, the splashing and thrashing only embed the hook even deeper in the fish's jaw.

Once a hook of sin has become embedded in us, we're also in for a battle. There's no way around it. Sin always involves a struggle, pain, and other negative consequences. Jesus said, "Most assuredly, I say to you, whoever commits sin is a slave of sin" (John 8:34). A slave in Jesus' time could win his freedom, but it was a very difficult thing to do.

When the first round of frantic thrashing doesn't work, a bass will sometimes make a run for it, hoping to escape by swimming as far away as possible, as quickly as possible. The fisherman may give the fish some line, but eventually the fish will come to the end of it. At that point, the fish is exhausted, and it's even easier to reel in.

Do we splash and thrash when our sexual sin is discovered? No question about it. Our splashing and thrashing often take the form of denial or justification—oh, how many excuses we make!

"Everybody does it."

"It's no big deal."

"It was only one time."

"It didn't mean anything."

"It was *only* sex—it wasn't love."

"We never actually *did* anything" [apart, that is, from writing letters, holding hands, kissing, meeting secretly, talking on the phone, and daydreaming together about what it would be like to be together in an even more intimate setting].

Splash, splash. Thrash, thrash.

We must never kid ourselves. Lust is a total-person sin. There's no such thing as "just a little sex." Sexual intercourse involves not only body parts, but all of a person's identity, emotions, and soul.

Some who commit sexual sin try to run. A person might take an extra-long business trip, change jobs, move to another city, or get an unlisted phone number. But eventually the person reaches the end of the line.

Once a person commits a sexual sin, it's much easier for that person to commit yet another act of sexual sin. This is true for all sin, but it seems especially true for sexual sin. The thinking is, *Well, I've already messed up in this area of my life and destroyed my purity [or lost my virginity or dented my fidelity], so why stop now?*

Anytime you find yourself on the line, hooked into yielding to temptation, the only way to snap the line is to ask the Lord to forgive you of your sin, to cleanse you of it, and to free you from its grip. And then, swim free! Refuse to yield to the temptation of biting that particular lure again.

We can be sure that Satan does not practice catch and release. He is after eternal victims. His goal is to keep a fish on the line until that fish is plopped into his bucket of water on the boat. And then he mounts his catch.

Believe me, Satan has amazing trophy rooms. He has all kinds of people mounted in his "lust" trophy room— people who are leaders of their community; people who are thought to be innocent, sweet, and totally pure; people who are pillars of the church. He has trophies of housewives, pastors, athletes, politicians—all caught by the lure of lust.

Satan is patient. He casts. He works the line. We bite

and fight. But he reels us in. Satan is willing to be patient because he knows the lure of lust works. He has been using it for centuries. Same ol' lure. Same ol' fishing technique. And, unfortunately, the same ol' hearts within the fish he goes after.

MAKING A PLAN TO STAY OFF THE HOOK

Bass are caught on lures twelve months a year. That's an amazing fact to me. It would seem that after a while, at least one of the more intelligent bass in the lake would think, *Hmmm. Every time one of my bass friends attacks one of those funny-looking things in the water, he is jerked out of the lake and is never seen again. Maybe I ought to think twice before lunging after one of those little skirtlike things with a bit of pork rind at its back.*

Are people any brighter when it comes to the lure of lust? We human beings never seem to learn.

If you don't develop a plan for staying away from the lure that the Ol' Angler casts in your direction, you will likely end up as one of his trophies.

I've noted several lust-busters that can help you stay off his hook.

Refrain from Flirtatious Comments and Gestures

A number of years ago, my wife, Lisa, and I counseled a couple who were planning to be married. The young man said to me, "Both my fiancée and I are very good at the art of flirting. She's a great flirt. So am I. People love it. They always enjoy having us around." The young woman giggled and added, "We love to tease."

On the way home that night, Lisa said to me, "They are in trouble. That relationship isn't going to last." And sure enough, a few months later they parted company.

Flirtatious comments and gestures convey the message, *I have more for you than what I am giving to you right now.* A flirtatious person continually invites, "Get to know me better. Even better. Yes, even better."

Any relationship that is truly valuable to you—and especially a relationship with a spouse—must have boundaries. Husband, your spouse is not just another woman. Wife, your spouse is not just another man. That person has been made "of one flesh" with you. If you are married, you have no authority to say, "Get to know my spouse better"—and yet that is what you are saying when you invite a person to get to know you better. Your marriage relationship is holy before God. It must be "set apart" from other people when it comes to sexual, intimate sharing.

Some people have said to me, "I'm just a huggy, touchy, smoochy type of person. My touching others doesn't really *mean* anything to me." Have you stopped to consider that although it doesn't mean anything to you, it may mean something to the person you are hugging, touching, or smooching?

You also don't know when your hugging, touching, smooching behavior might ignite something in you. It's like being a habitual match lighter. Most of the time the things you light don't spark into a roaring fire—but there just may be a time when you light the fuse of a bomb or get that match too close to an open gallon of gasoline. The accidental explosion is just as real as if you had intended it. "But I was just lighting a match," you may say. Too late. The match found a source of fuel that was more combustible than what you could handle.

Being a hugging, touching, smooching type of person isn't bad—just be that type of person with your spouse.

Guard Your Eyes

Retrain your eyes to see what is good for you to look at, not only what is good-looking.

Samson was born with more potential and more leadership skills than just about any other person in the Bible except Jesus Christ. Even before his birth, Samson was singled out by God for a destiny of greatness. He was given prime opportunities for helping Israel to step up to the next level in becoming the nation God desired it to be. But, he was a biblical bodybuilder who was a he-man with a "she" weakness.

You might assume that the first words attributed to Samson in the Bible would be noble words, such as, "Let's get it together, Israelites, and really make a difference," or "Let's discipline ourselves and take this country into the next zone. We can do it—this is our year." Not so. The first words attributed to Samson are, "I have seen a woman" (Judg. 14:2). Those words plagued Samson all his life.

There is no mention of Samson's knowing anything about this first woman other than that she was one of the Philistines, who were the archenemies of Israel. There is no mention of her personality, her character, or her spiritual traits. Samson merely "saw" her. He let his wandering eye dwell on her with lust. And on the basis of his lust alone, he wanted her as a wife.

Samson had known *from birth* that God had chosen him to be a leader and that he was to marry a godly Israelite girl. Samson knew right from wrong, and he chose wrong. First, he wanted the Philistine girl of Timnah, next, a Philistine harlot in Gaza, and then, a Philistine woman named Delilah. By the time Samson got to Delilah, he was completely ruled by lust.

You know the story. He got a haircut in a Toni and Guy Salon by this beautiful stylist named Delilah and after she cut his hair, he lost his strength, his charisma, his creativity, his leadership, and his freedom. He is one of the greatest examples in the Bible of "what might have been."

Samson, of course, is not the only victim of lust in the Bible. In each and every case where lust played a part in a person's life, the results were devastating.

David gave in to his lust for Bathsheba. He continued to look long after he should have turned away. And what did it cost him? The near loss of his throne, the sexual misbehavior of his children, the rape of his daughter, the death of an infant son, and eventually the deaths of two of his older sons. The price was extremely high for David.

Solomon traded in commitment to God's commandments for political maneuvering. He took hundreds of women to be his wives and concubines. The result? A cynical attitude toward life, an empty heart, and an empire ripe for division.

No good thing comes from misplaced sexual passion.

Look Past the Lure of Lust to the Consequences

Anytime you feel a lustful desire, train yourself to focus immediately upon the consequences of sexual sin:

- emotional turmoil and guilt;
- divorce or marital estrangement;
- disease—including deadly disease;
- estrangement from family and friends;
- loss—psychological and, in many cases, physical, financial, and spiritual;
- damage to one's reputation;
- pain and heartache—initially perhaps to others, but ultimately to oneself; and
- emotional and spiritual death.

James wrote, "When desire has conceived, it gives birth to sin; and sin, when it is full-grown, brings forth death" (James 1:15). James was speaking of emotional and spiritual death.

The person who gives in to lustful temptation has forgotten the consequences that might be associated with fornication and adultery. In case you don't know or have forgotten what is forbidden by God, let me remind you. We are commanded not to engage in:

- *fornication*, which is sexual intercourse between two unmarried people.

- *adultery*, which is sexual intercourse between two people, at least one of whom is married to another person.

- *incest*, which is sexual intercourse between two people who are closely related and for whom sexual intercourse has been prohibited by God.

- *homosexuality*, which is sexual intercourse between two people of the same sex.

- *bestiality*, which is sexual intercourse between a human being and an animal. (See Ex. 22:19; Lev. 18:6–23; 20:6–21.)

Some words associated with these sexual sins are *abomination, abhorrent*, and *defilement*. That's as strong as the Bible can get in condemning something. The biblical punishment for such sins was severe, including banishment and death.

Sexual intercourse was and is reserved for people who are married. God has been very clear on the boundaries related to sex.

The Bible also tells us that the Christian who commits an immoral sexual act has taken Christ into that very act with him. Paul wrote, "He who is joined to the Lord is one spirit with Him" (1 Cor. 6:17). Paul also said, "Do you not know that your bodies are members of Christ? Shall I then take the members of Christ and make them members of a harlot? Certainly not!" (1 Cor. 6:15).

To engage in sexual sin is to severely damage one's relationship with the Lord.

Run from the Obvious Opportunity

Anytime a person other than your spouse makes a sexual advance toward you, run. Put some distance between yourself and that other person. Stay away from the person. Avoid the person. Refuse ever to be alone with the person.

As I mentioned in an earlier chapter, Joseph's brothers sold Joseph into slavery in a fit of anger and jealousy. Joseph eventually found himself working in the house of Potiphar, the head of Egypt's CIA. Potiphar saw Joseph's great potential and trusted the top management position of his estate to Joseph.

Potiphar had his choice of all the women in Egypt, and

he picked one who was not known for her good personality, if you know what I mean. She was a provocative, seductive woman. For his part, Joseph was very attractive. The Bible says he was "handsome in form and appearance."

There's nothing wrong with being good-looking. Joseph is the innocent person in this story. I will warn those of you who are good-looking, however, that good looks make you a prime target for more lures of lust to be cast in your direction.

Potiphar's wife looked at Joseph with lustful eyes, but she didn't stop there. She brazenly said, "Lie with me" (Gen. 39:7).

When Mrs. Potiphar made her first advance toward Joseph, he refused her. He said, in our terms today, "Ma'am, I could do what you ask, and nobody would know. The problem is, ma'am, God would know. And I can't sin against God."

Good response. But Mrs. Potiphar didn't give up. She continued to tempt him "day by day." And day by day, Joseph refused her. Then came the day when all of the other servants were outside the house and Mrs. Potiphar not only said, "Lie with me," but also grabbed Joseph's clothes and pulled him toward her. The Bible tells us that Joseph made a fifty-yard dash for the door and never looked back to take his coat (Gen. 39:11–12).

When Mrs. Potiphar realized Joseph was never going to give in to her, she called some of the servants and lied and said Joseph had put the moves on her and she was the one who had barely escaped being raped. Unfortunately she had his garment in her hand, and that seemed to prove her point. Her lie landed Joseph in a dungeon.

When you refuse a person who attempts to seduce you, you may be cast out. Your name may be maligned, your reputation may be dented by lies, and you may be left off the A-party invitation list. So be it.

Teenagers, as well as college students and other young adults, who refuse to engage in sexual behavior may be called names. Being a virgin may be frowned upon, ridiculed, or laughed at. The person who is pure may be made to feel weird. So be it.

Ultimately the opinions of others aren't going to count. It's what *God* says and what *God* requires that count.

God didn't forget Joseph in that dungeon, and He won't forget you if you suffer negative consequences for turning down an offer of sexual sin. It took a little while, but God eventually elevated Joseph into a position in which he was number two only to Pharaoh and significantly higher in rank than Potiphar!

Some of us need to be running from certain people and certain places. Always remember: As long as you are running from lustful temptations, you can't fall victim to them. God honors those who keep His commandments.

Monitor Your Media Intake
Each of us is bombarded each month with thousands of messages that have heavy sexual content. Newspapers,

magazines, books, billboards, radio programs, music, television, movies—the lure of lust seems to be everywhere.

An article in *U.S. News & World Report,* February 10, 1997, stated that in one year alone, Americans spent $8 billion on hard-core videos, peep shows, live sex acts, adult cable programming, computer pornography, sexual devices, and sex magazines. This amount is far greater than Hollywood's domestic movie box-office receipts and also larger than all of the revenues generated by country and rock music recordings. That's staggering!

Americans spend more money at strip clubs each year than they do in purchasing tickets for Broadway, off-Broadway, regional, and nonprofit theaters, and for opera, ballet, jazz, and classical music performances *combined.* We have more laws related to the production of sexually explicit materials than any other Western industrialized nation, and yet we produce a much greater quantity of pornographic materials than any other nation—a whopping 150 new "titles" a week.

It's time to run! It's time to turn our eyes away from the media of our culture. It's time to turn off all forms of input that deal with corruption.

We need to do what Job did. He said,

> I have made a covenant with my eyes;
> Why then should I look upon a young woman?
> For what is the allotment of God from above,
> And the inheritance of the Almighty from on high?

> Is it not destruction for the wicked,
> And disaster for the workers of iniquity?
> Does He not see my ways,
> And count all my steps? (Job 31:1–4)

Job made a covenant—not as the lure was about to sink into him, not after the fact, not in retrospect as he looked back over his life. Job made a covenant with his eyes *before* temptation came. Why? Because he feared God's judgment more than he desired to sin.

As Christians, we don't need to watch some sitcoms, go to some movies, read certain magazines or novels, or click on to some Web sites.

What you see and hear, what you take into your mind, and what you entertain in your imagination become what you think about. The more you think about something, the more likely you are to act on the thought. This is not only true for lust—it's true for all sin. The more you think about acts of revenge, the more you are likely to engage in vengeance. The more you think about stealing something, acting violently, eating something that is bad for you, or taking drugs, the more likely you are to steal, be violent, pig out on junk food, or experiment with drugs. The more you think about sexual behavior, the more you are likely to engage in sexual behavior.

The filter you need is given in Philippians 4:8. Focus your mind, Paul said, on what is true, noble, just, pure, lovely, and good.

You may be saying, "But, Ed, this R-rated movie I want to see only has a couple of questionable scenes, and I can handle that. Seeing a little bit of skin won't affect me." Who are you trying to kid? Those questionable scenes may get stuck in your mind and fuel lust in you for weeks. It's far better to shut off all scenes that you know to be of questionable nature than to have one of those scenes linger in your mind and cause you to stumble.

Some of us need to clean out the magazines by the bed and throw away some of the videos we have purchased. It's time to clean house and clean up our thinking.

Maximize Your Marriage

The best defense is a good offense. This isn't true only in sports. It's also true when it comes to sexual behavior. One of the most powerful things you can do to avoid the lure of lust is to maximize the sexual dimension of your marriage. God created sex. He said to keep a lovely thing lovely. He wants full sexual intimacy to be enjoyed in the fully committed relationship called marriage.

Paul offered this marriage advice: "Do not deprive one another except with consent for a time, that you may give yourselves to fasting and prayer; and come together again so that Satan does not tempt you because of your lack of self-control" (1 Cor. 7:5). In other words, do your best to satisfy the needs of your partner, and in return, choose to be satisfied fully by your partner.

Can't you just imagine the new excuse? It will no

longer be, "Honey, I have a headache." It will be, "Honey, I have a need to pray." Prayer isn't to be an excuse for refusing sex to a mate! Agreement about refraining from sex is necessary. From time to time, a couple might agree together to refrain from sex in order to fast and pray about something, but once that season of fasting and prayer has ended, they are to resume normal marital relations.

Sometimes a spouse may say no. It may come from either the wife or the husband. There are legitimate reasons for *not* engaging in sexual behavior at certain times. But let me give you this practical advice: If you are going to say no to your spouse, do so with an appointment. Say, "No, not tonight, but tomorrow morning or tomorrow night."

I once asked for my congregation to respond to this question with a show of hands: "How many of you have preschoolers in your home?" Well over half of the hands in the congregation went up. I immediately led the congregation in a moment of silence for those husbands and wives, in part because that moment in church may have been the only moment of silence they had in weeks! If you have young children in your home, your sex life is going to suffer. You need to make time for your spouse.

Don't let anything wear out all of your emotional and physical energy. Not your job. Not young children. Not commitments to friends, social engagements, clubs, organizations, or even church volunteer work. Make an effort to keep romance and sexual vibrancy alive in your marriage.

To keep from striking the lure of lust, have a satisfying sexual relationship with your spouse. Work on it. In recalling our fishing analogy—well-fed fish don't need the bait offered by a fisherman.

Establish Accountability

I believe accountability is especially important for men. Countless men carry around sexual secrets and fantasies. They struggle with lust, but have no outlet for discussing their struggle. Many men are too embarrassed to admit that they harbor lustful desires, that they have been involved with pornography in the past, or that someone at work or at the gym seems intent on seducing them.

Each of us needs to be able to confide struggles with temptations of all kinds to another Christian. This is especially important in regard to lust. Admitting lust is one of the best ways to defuse it, but don't just talk about the lust you feel. Receive the prayers and support and wise counsel of the person in whom you confide. Find strength in accountability.

The person to whom you are accountable should be a person of your same sex. Ideally this person should be older than you and should have a deep love for God and an understanding of the Bible. You should feel confident that this person will be loyal to you and keep your conversations private. You must be able to rely on this person for availability and honesty.

Don't seek out a person who frequents topless clubs or tells off-color jokes or brags about this sexual conquest or that sexual conquest. You must avoid talking to this fellow about your sexual temptations!

The person to whom you can talk about your sexual temptations may be willing to listen to other kinds of temptations that the Ol' Angler dangles in front of you. A strong Christian accountability partner is an extremely valuable person to have in your life. I strongly encourage you to develop this relationship.

The person in whom I confide is someone I can call on the phone at a moment's notice and say, "Hey, I'm struggling with this. Pray with me about it. Give me your advice on this." Through the years, this person has been as influential as any other mentor, friend, teacher, parent, or wise counselor in my life when it comes to helping me grow as a person.

Proverbs 27:17 stresses that "as iron sharpens iron, so a man sharpens the countenance of his friend." My accountability partner is like iron sharpening me. He helps sharpen me into a tool that the Lord can use more effectively.

I have caught myself saying in the past, "I wish God would just take temptation away. *Boom*—gone. A done deal. Why do we have to deal with all this temptation anyway? Why can't we just say no once and be finished with temptation for all time?"

James 1:12 gives the answer: "Blessed is the man who endures temptation; for when he has been approved, he will receive the crown of life which the Lord has promised to those who love Him." Temptation can lead to seduction and demise, or it can lead to strength and reward. Temptation results in either destruction or development. The choice is ours.

When we say no to temptation, our faith is built up. We develop resistance to evil. Our character and integrity grow.

If we want to grow into greatness and spiritual maturity, we are going to have to say no to a lot of lures in our lives, including the lure of lust. The biggest bass in the lake gets that way by following one technique: It avoids the hooks thrown its way.

WHAT ABOUT LUST'S IMPACT ON WOMEN?

Are men the only ones who struggle with lust and fall victim to it? No. Women, however, seem to be better at hiding this sin from others.

Some think that the profile of a lustful woman is a prostitute. I suspect very few prostitutes are motivated by lust. They use the images of lust to get what they want, just as Delilah did. Delilah wasn't motivated by lust or love. She was motivated by the offer of a large sum of money from several Philistine lords. She then used lustful means to get to Samson.

What is the profile, then, of a lustful woman? She sees every man as a potential lover. She fantasizes about sex with every man to whom she feels any kind of attraction. She thinks about the husbands of friends, the men who work at her home as repairmen or gardeners, the men who star on TV soap operas, and the men who are romanticized in dime-store novels.

"But," you may say, "women want love, not sex. They use sex to get love, while men give love to get sex." That's a well-known statement, and there's some truth in it. There are also women who enjoy sex and never seem to get enough of it. If you are a woman, don't think you are immune from the sin of lust.

In many cases, a woman desires primarily a feeling of closeness with a man. She enjoys the comfort of a hug and a kiss, and the feelings of safety and belonging that come from sitting close to someone. This desire for closeness is a prime ingredient of romance. Ask a woman if she desires romance, and she generally says, "You bet!"

In many ways, romance is lust with feminine frills. It brings out all of the passions and feelings and behaviors that more racy and raw forms of lustful temptation evoke in men.

Don't be fooled by a preoccupation with romance. The end of the romantic tale is not only that the couple live happily ever after. Someplace along the line you are going to find heavy breathing, passionate kissing, and a highly volatile romp in the hay. And with anybody other than a husband, that's sexual sin.

MAKING A COMMITMENT TO SEXUAL PURITY

I suspect that a very high percentage of Christians have never made a commitment to the Lord that involves lust or their sex life. They have never said to the Lord, "I commit myself to purity and to keeping Your commandments about sex. I commit myself to saying no to lustful desires, sexual fantasies, and flirtatious behavior with anyone other than my spouse. I commit myself to doing things Your way."

People have said to me, "Ed, I want to be good in this area. I'm trying to be better about this. I don't want to sin too much in this area." That's like a soldier going into battle and saying, "I don't want to get shot too much."

A commitment about sexual purity and right sexual behavior is not a commitment we can make on a sliding scale. It's all-or-nothing. Either we commit to being celibate as a single person, and faithful as a married person, or we don't.

ACCEPT GOD'S OFFER OF FORGIVENESS FOR SEXUAL SIN

Jesus seemed to have had a special love for people who got caught in sexual sin. One day He met a Samaritan woman. She had been married five times and was then living with a guy to whom she was not married. She came to draw water from the town well, and Jesus offered her the "living water" of God's love and forgiveness (John 4:1–42).

Another time, a woman caught in the act of adultery was brought to Jesus. She was on the verge of being stoned by the church leaders. Jesus said to her, "Neither do I condemn you; go and sin no more" (John 8:2–11).

Jesus allowed a woman of ill repute—very likely a prostitute—to wash His feet with her tears, wipe them with her hair, and then anoint them with fragrant oil. When He was criticized for permitting this, He turned the table on His critics. He essentially said to the woman, "Your sins, which are many, are forgiven. Go in peace." (See Luke 7:36–50.)

I want you to see four things in these examples from the Gospels:

1. *Jesus didn't deny the presence of sexual sin.* He never said, "Oh, that's not important. There are bigger issues in life." Sexual sin *is* important, it does matter, and it is a big deal. Everybody may be doing it, but everybody who is engaging in sexual sin is also wrong. Jesus never winked at sexual sin.

2. *Jesus was willing to confront people about their sin.* He didn't turn and walk away from sinners. He didn't let the woman at the well draw her water and return to her serial-marriage lifestyle without confronting her with God's love. You must be equally bold in calling sin what it is: sin.

3. *Jesus had great compassion for sinners.* He did not condemn any of these three women. He showed compassion

for them. He received them into His presence. No matter how great or how public their sin, He forgave them.

4. Jesus told those who had sinned to "sin no more." His forgiveness was not a license to continue to sin. His forgiveness gave them the courage *not* to sin again in this area. The people He forgave were set free from lust's hook so they might swim free—and swim as far away from the lure of temptation as possible.

When it comes to your sin, no matter what you have done or are doing, Jesus wants to set you free too. He knows your sin, and He will continue to confront you about it. The best thing you can do is to face up to your sin, admit it, and let Jesus forgive you and restore your relationship with God. You can also count on Jesus saying to you, "Go and sin no more."

It is your responsibility to receive God's forgiveness—to accept it and be grateful for it and forgive yourself. It's your responsibility not to dwell on your past sins or continue to beat yourself up over them. It is also your responsibility to change your behavior. You must choose not to sin again.

CHOOSE TO BREAK FREE

No matter how many times you may have fallen into temptation and yielded to sin, you can still come to the

Father and receive His forgiveness and make a fresh start in your life.

No matter how many affairs you may have had or how long you've been in a sinful relationship, you can break that pattern of sin. You can put a stop to that relationship and begin again to walk a path of sexual purity before the Lord.

No matter how many times you may have failed in the past, you don't need to sin in this area again.

Choose to break free of the bondage of lust. Ask the Lord to help you daily to put the big chill on all undesirable desires!

GLUTTONY

Taking the Giant out of Giant-Sized

When I was in high school, my father attempted an impossible mission—he tried to teach me how to drive. My first and only lesson with him lasted a couple of hours. Finally he threw up his hands and said, "Ed, I don't have enough patience for this. I'm not trained for this. I'm going to get someone to help you learn to drive."

The next day after school, a car pulled up in our driveway, and on it was a sign: TONY SELLERS EASY METHOD DRIVER TRAINING SCHOOL. Tony Sellers himself got out of the car, and after introductions, he informed me that he had been hired to teach me to drive. I said, "Fine," and he said, "Let's go."

Immediately he put me behind the wheel, and off we went, straight for the freeway. He didn't waste a minute. I was driving on the freeway, a little nervous, with my hands on the steering wheel at the ten and two positions. Things were going all right, so I decided to change lanes. I looked in the rearview mirror and into the side mirror and began to make my move. Suddenly a car began to honk: *Beep! Beep! Beep!* I had almost run someone off the road. A car had been in my blind spot.

Tony grabbed the wheel and shouted, "What are you doing?" He got us to safety, and we headed home. I apologized to Mr. Sellers repeatedly for almost destroying his car and possibly killing him. He responded with some words I've never forgotten: "Ed, there are blind spots in driving every car. In fact, many accidents occur because drivers forget about the blind spots." To this day, I am very cautious when it comes to changing lanes and making turns. I'm alert for blind spots.

A blind spot. An area that's easily overlooked. A situation that can cause a deadly crash. The truth isn't limited to cars and driving—it's a truth that applies to every area of our lives, especially to sin.

For many people, gluttony is a major blind spot. They do not see gluttony for the sin that it is. Oh, they realize they may be overweight. They may admit they find great pleasure in eating. But they would never in a million years classify their self-indulgence as a sin. "After all," they say, "junk food isn't the same as drugs!"

WHAT EXACTLY IS GLUTTONY?

Gluttony is taking into your body more than your body needs. The Bible describes two types of excess:

1. Food. "A fool when he is filled with food" is considered a person who brings great trouble to the world (Prov. 30:21–22).

2. Drink. Proverbs 20:1 warns against excess in drinking:

> Wine is a mocker,
> Strong drink is a brawler,
> And whoever is led astray by it is not wise.

Overindulging in too much rich food and too much strong drink is equated with prodigal living, or wanton living. We find this in the story of the prodigal son. The Bible describes such a lifestyle as a "waste" (Luke 15:13–14). It is also a lifestyle that eventually results in our being "wasted"—things that are truly important to us are lost.

To the glutton, consuming food and drink becomes more important than strengthening family relationships, serving God, working, paying bills, and even sleeping. What is consumed becomes more important than any obligation or responsibility that is a typical part of life. The addiction to sugar, alcohol, fat, or any other substance taken into the body becomes the focus of life.

Gluttons are those who live to eat and drink rather than eat and drink to live.

Our National Problem with Gluttony

A large percentage of people in our nation, including the church, struggle with gluttony.

In the United States, some seven million people are classified as severely obese, nearly thirteen million are obese, and eighty million are overweight. In other words, nearly half of the population of the United States of America has a weight problem. Medical experts estimate that about 10 percent of this group have genetic factors related to their weight. The other 90 percent are overweight because they eat more calories than they burn as body heat. They are obese because they let themselves be obese.

Are you aware that in the United States, the average person eats in one day the calories that most of the people around the world eat in a week? The average caloric intake for the world as a whole is 436 calories per person per day. The average caloric intake per person in the USA is 3,576 calories per day.

Are you aware that the average American adult consumes 129 pounds of sugar a year, and the average American teenager eats or drinks 400 pounds of sugar a year? We eat an average of 52 teaspoons of fat and 6 to 7 teaspoons of salt a day! Mix the two in a bowl and you'll have a tough time getting the spoon out of the mixture, much less get that mixture out of your arteries.

I have to laugh at times when I go out to eat with friends. The waitress delivers orders of superdeluxe nachos, chicken-fried steaks smothered in gravy, and a loaded baked potato or two, and then we have the audacity to say, "Let's pray." We ask God to "bless this food to the nourishment of our bodies." Do we truly expect God to answer that prayer?

Some of us struggle because we like the taste of certain foods and beverages. Some of us struggle because we have never learned how to eat right. But some of us struggle with gluttony because of deeper issues—it may be poor self-esteem, a relational problem, anger, or stress. These people eat to feel better emotionally. Eating is only a temporary fix, not a solution.

Like all of the fatal distractions, gluttony has land mines that blow up in our faces. If we seek out food to help us feel better about ourselves and to give us more esteem, we are going to eat or drink ourselves into a position where we feel even *less* esteem. If we seek out food to comfort us when we are angry or sad, we can eat or drink ourselves right into a state of feeling even sadder or angrier. If we eat out of stress, we are probably going to get even more stressed out about the way we look and feel when we get fatter.

Gluttony is the one fatal distraction that a person cannot hide. It's there for all the world to see. It results in poor health and very often serious health risks.

Obesity vs. Gluttony

Not only overweight people can be gluttons. In fact, a person can be thin and be a glutton.

Gluttony is making food more important than obeying God. Gluttony occurs when eating and drinking are of greater interest, purpose, meaning, pleasure, and concern than obeying God. Gluttony is turning to food for comfort, recreation, and satisfaction rather than turning to the Lord to supply emotional needs.

What about the pencil-thin model? What about the person who is an exercise junkie—who can't work out enough? What about the person who suffers from anorexia nervosa or bulimia?

Excessive dieting is like the flip side of the same coin called gluttony. Compulsive dieters are just as concerned about food as those who eat all the time and become obese. An overwhelming concern with food makes a person a glutton, not the number on the scale.

Gluttony is the sin of being preoccupied with the temporary state of one's physical being. The opposite of gluttony is having a concern for the eternal state of the soul. Philippians 3:19 describes the enemies of the cross of Christ as those "whose god is their belly, and whose glory is in their shame—who set their mind on earthly things." The Roman world was known for gluttony—orgies to the point that the people forced themselves to vomit so they could eat and drink even more. They lived to have their taste buds and their senses tickled. They were totally engrossed with self-gratification.

And that's what is deadly about gluttony. It puts all the focus on self, self, self . . . now, now, now. A gluttonous person is totally self-focused. There is no room for God. There is no thought, *What would Jesus do?*

I challenge you to face some tough questions:

- How much time do you spend thinking about food?

- How often do you talk about what you weigh, either too much or too little?

- Are you ever more concerned about your next meal than about the next time you read your Bible?

- Are you more concerned about getting out of the office and to a restaurant before the noon rush than you are about getting to church on time next Sunday?

- Are you more concerned about how much you weigh than about how much time you are spending in prayer?

- Do you spend more of your day preparing food, thinking about food, shopping for food, and eating food than you do in spiritually related activities?

- Are you more aware of fast-food commercials,

billboards, and restaurants than opportunities to help people in need?

If the answer is even a reluctant "maybe" to any of these questions, you must take seriously the issue of gluttony.

WHY IS GLUTTONY A DEADLY SIN?

Everywhere we turn in our culture we are bombarded by messages that cry out, "Try this! You can't eat just one! Here, have a whole bag of whatever it is you desire!" We live in the ultimate consumer society on this earth. What we see, we want. What we want, we take. What we take, we take again and again. The word we live by seems to be *more!*

Paul wrote to Timothy about a man named Demas, saying that Demas had forsaken him, "having loved this present world" (2 Tim. 4:10). Gluttony is bound to this earth and to what is part of the natural world. The glutton sees only what is before him. He fails to see the big picture of eternity. He fails to place the proper priority on spiritual matters and on the Lord's work.

A glutton spends most of his time thinking about what to eat, what to drink, where to shop, what to buy, what to enjoy, and what to experience. Gluttony is putting the things of this world before the things of God. It is a form of idolatry. You may not have thought of too many trips to your favorite fast-food restaurant as a form of idolatry, but if you make consumption your god, you make what you consume an idol.

Stop to consider for a moment:

- How many more souls could be saved if all of the money spent on late-night snacks was given to missionaries?

- How much could be accomplished in the spirit realm if people used half of every lunch hour to read the Word or pray?

- What might be done for the gospel if the $10 billion that is spent each year on diet pills, powders, liquids, and nutrient bars was funneled into ministry?

What God Says About Gluttony in the Bible

Anywhere gluttony is mentioned in the Scriptures, we find harsh words. Eliphaz, one of Job's friends, described the *wicked* obese man as one who "has covered his face with his fatness, and made his waist heavy with fat" (Job 15:27). The sin of the wicked man was not obesity itself, but the fact that he was totally self-centered in his consumption.

Proverbs 23:21 tells us, "The drunkard and the glutton will come to poverty." Why? Not because they are alcoholic or fat, but because they are more concerned about consuming than about working.

The Bible paints several vivid pictures of gluttons. One of these portraits appears in the book of Amos:

Woe to you who put far off the day of doom,
Who cause the seat of violence to come near;
Who lie on beds of ivory,
Stretch out on your couches,
Eat lambs from the flock
And calves from the midst of the stall;
Who sing idly to the sound of stringed instruments,
And invent for yourselves musical instruments
    like David;
Who drink wine from bowls,
And anoint yourselves with the best ointments,
But are not grieved for the affliction of Joseph.
Therefore they shall now go captive as the
    first of the captives,
And those who recline at banquets shall be removed.
(Amos 6:3–7)

Gluttony was directly related to the death of Eli's sons (1 Sam. 2:12–17). Gluttony caused the Jews to lust after Egypt and to long to return there (Num. 11:4–6). The Law of Moses even called for a son who was a glutton and a drunkard to be stoned to death (Deut. 21:20–21)!

The First Cousins of Gluttony
One reason that gluttony is so deadly is that it is

closely related to some other things God hates: pride, a lack of trust, and covetousness.

Pride. Belshazzar was an eat-drink-and-be-merry kind of guy. As king, he ordered an elaborate feast for a thousand of his top managers. During the wine-tasting part of the feast, Belshazzar gave a command to bring out all of the gold and silver vessels that his father had taken from the temple in Jerusalem. He was obviously showing off. But then he distributed the sacred vessels to his lords, wives, and concubines so they could drink wine from them and praise their own Babylonian gods of gold, silver, bronze, iron, wood, and stone.

That same hour the fingers of a man's hand mysteriously appeared and wrote on the plaster wall of the king's palace. Daniel was brought in to interpret the writing, and the message was devastating: "You have not humbled your heart, although you knew from your father the power of God. God has taken account of your kingdom, and it is at an end. God has weighed you in His balances of justice, and you are found wanting. Your kingdom is going to be divided among your enemies." That very night Belshazzar was killed. (See Dan. 5.)

Pride causes the glutton to decide he can eat and drink whatever he likes, in any manner he chooses, without any consequences before God. Pride causes a person to conclude, "My body is my own. I can put into it anything and use it in any way I desire." As Christians, we do *not* belong to ourselves. We belong to Christ.

A lack of trust. After the resurrection and ascension of Christ, the followers of Christ were on a high spiritually. At the same time, their bank accounts and reputations hit bottom. Many were rejected by their families and friends. Many lost their homes and their businesses.

The new Christians didn't let those problems stop them. They pulled together and pooled their resources and kept worshiping Jesus as their Savior (Acts 2:44–45).

Two of the early believers were Ananias and Sapphira. They sold a piece of property, brought *part* of the money to Peter, and told Peter that they were giving *all* of the money to the new community of Christians. They lied, and Peter knew it instantly. He basically said to Ananias, "It was your possession. You didn't have to sell it. And even after you sold it, you could have done with the money what you wanted. Why have you lied to us and to God about this?" When Ananias heard these words, he fell down dead at Peter's feet.

Sapphira came along a few hours later. Peter asked her about the money. She lied, too, and when she was confronted, she also fell down dead (Acts 5:1–11).

What does this story have to do with gluttony? Ananias and Sapphira were not willing to sell all to follow the Lord. They kept part of the control over their lives and their finances for themselves. Then they lied about their gift, claiming to have surrendered all, even though they hadn't surrendered all.

The glutton says, "All of me for Christ," and at the

same time, he reserves for himself the right to put into his body whatever he wants, in whatever quantities he wants.

The issue is one of trust. Whom will you trust with your body? Do you trust the Lord to provide your next meal and your next breath? Or do you believe you must consume everything in sight because you might not have enough tomorrow?

Covetousness. Another first cousin of gluttony is covetousness. The glutton wants not only his portion but also another person's portion. King Ahab had that feeling about Naboth's vineyard. Naboth's vineyard was right next door to Ahab's palace, and Ahab thought it might be a good piece of ground for a vegetable garden. He offered to buy the vineyard, but Naboth replied, "No way! I'm not about to give my inheritance to you!"

Ahab was upset and started pouting over Naboth's response—even to the point of going to his bed and refusing to eat. So Jezebel, Ahab's wife, took matters into her hands. She arranged to have Naboth killed on trumped-up charges, and then she insisted that Ahab take over the property after Naboth was dead. The end result was a bloody, horrible death for Jezebel and a serious wake-up scare for Ahab. (See 1 Kings 21.)

The glutton is never satisfied with what God provides—he is always craving another bite, another sip, another moment of self-indulgence. The glutton lives for what he can enjoy and savor and consume. And the end is deadly for both body and soul.

PUTTING A CONCERN FOR OUR BODIES INTO PERSPECTIVE

To what extent should we be concerned about our bodies? Is God concerned about our physical nature? Where should the boundary lines be drawn?

God's Concern About Our Physical Bodies

God is very concerned about our physical authenticity. He wants us to be strong, healthy, and vibrant, with enough energy and endurance to go the distance. He does not want us to be obsessive about food or about our physical bodies, however. The Bible sets forth several truths about God's relationship to our physical bodies.

God made us. Genesis 2:7 informs us that "the LORD God formed man of the dust of the ground, and breathed into his nostrils the breath of life; and man became a living being." God was vitally and intimately involved with our bodies from the very beginning. Our transcendent God took dust in His fingers, molded it in His hands, and shaped us. We are tailor-made, custom designed, and one of a kind. We are God's masterpieces.

I'll never forget the day my wife, Lisa, put a camera

in my office while I was out a while. She focused the camera on my office chair. When I returned to my office, I found her there. I sat down, and she said, "Ed, I just got back from the doctor. He did a sonogram, and here is the heartbeat of Baby A." I said, "Great!" And then it hit me, *Baby A?*

Lisa went on, "Here is the heartbeat of Baby B." I stuttered, "Twins?" As I looked at the little pictures of the sonogram, I thought about the great miracle, the customized job that God performs when He creates us. She got my entire reaction on videotape. Anytime I need a reminder that God is directly and wonderfully involved in our lives from our conception until our homegoing to heaven, I pop in that tape.

God maintains our lives. Jesus taught, "Look at the birds of the air, for they neither sow nor reap nor gather into barns; yet your heavenly Father feeds them. Are you not of more value than they?" (Matt. 6:26).

If you are looking for an exciting Bible study, I invite you to read the book of Luke and highlight every time Jesus touched someone, healed someone, or ministered to someone. God desires to sustain and maintain and fulfill life.

When Jesus raised the little daughter of Jairus back to life, the first thing He said to her mother was, "Get the girl something to eat." Jesus sustains us. He is concerned about our health and vitality.

God wore flesh. God knows all about our physical needs. God, in the form of Jesus Christ, put on flesh (John 1:14). He wore skin. He lived within a human body. If anybody understands the aches, pains, and frailty of the human body, God does!

Several years ago, I was the chaplain of the Houston Astros. I'm not a big baseball fan, but I enjoyed the time with the team. A major-league all-star player came to me one afternoon and gave me two pairs of his game cleats. I took them home and wore them to mow the lawn. A friend of mine who was a baseball fanatic saw me and said, "Ed, are you mowing the lawn in those shoes? Those are from the Astros!" He even named the player whose number was on the side of the shoes. I said, "Sure. This is about the only reason I have to wear cleats. I have another pair just like them inside." This guy was so in awe of the shoes that I gave the second pair to him. He acted as if I had given him $10 million.

Why was he so excited about the shoes that a major-league ballplayer had worn a couple of times? They had a few grass stains and a little dirt and a number painted on them. But they were like gold to him. He was so fired up about them because a major-league all-star had "dignified" those shoes.

Jesus Christ dignified the human body. He wore flesh.

God dwells within us. The moment we receive Jesus Christ into our lives, the Holy Spirit of God dwells inside us for eternity. Paul said, "Do you not know that you are the temple of God and that the Spirit of God dwells in you?" (1 Cor. 3:16). The Holy Spirit chooses to live within human flesh—clay vessels called human bodies. What an awesome truth!

Paul added these words:

Do you not know that your body is the temple of the Holy Spirit who is in you, whom you have from God, and you are not your own? For you were bought at a price; therefore glorify God in your body and in your spirit, which are God's. (1 Cor. 6:19–20)

The Old Testament has a number of passages about the glory of God filling the tabernacle in the wilderness and, later, the temple in Jerusalem. Paul informed the Christians that God had moved. He was no longer in the tabernacle or the temple. He set up residence in our human bodies. He lives in us.

Before we had children, Lisa and I went to Israel, and while we were there, we toured Bethlehem and visited the Church of the Nativity where many archaeologists and scholars believe Jesus was born. That church in Bethlehem is one of the most valuable buildings on the planet. You couldn't buy it if you tried. Why is it worth so much? Because people have concluded that Jesus may have spent a few hours of His life on that spot of ground.

When it comes to your body, Jesus isn't just passing through. He is not on a long weekend visit. He has set up permanent residence in you in the form of the Holy Spirit. He is planning on living with you for all eternity. He values your body as His home.

God will resurrect our bodies. We get into a dangerous game every time we try to separate the body from the soul. Both are a vital part of our identity. In heaven, we will have perfected, glorified bodies. People will recognize us. They will know us not because they sense our particular atoms and energy patterns floating around, but because they will see us in bodies. We are going to have bodies that are just like the body Jesus Christ had after His resurrection (1 Cor. 15:40, 49).

I can hardly wait for that glorified body. Who knows? In heaven, I might have a vertical jump of two hundred feet!

God's Expectations About Our Physical Health and Fitness

What does God expect from us when it comes to our bodies?

We are to glorify God with our bodies. Paul said, "Glorify God in your body and in your spirit" (1 Cor. 6:20). We are to bring praise to God by the way we treat ourselves, including the way we treat our bodies.

We treat our churches reverently—we treat them in a holy, dignified manner. We take good care of our church facilities.

We should give the same treatment to our bodies. Do

we abuse our bodies? Do we tear our bodies down? Do we maintain them well?

Suppose someone walked into your office tomorrow morning and handed you the keys to a brand-new Ferrari F40. That particular model can hit speeds of more than two hundred miles per hour, and it retails for about $550,000. Now suppose the person hands the car keys to you and says, "This is my gift to you. I've paid for the car, and I've already paid in advance for the insurance and for all the gasoline you'll need. There's only one thing I ask—use only super unleaded fuel. If you put anything other than super unleaded in this car, it will slowly ruin the engine."

You'd probably respond, "Come on, man, I wouldn't think about putting regular unleaded or anything else in this machine. No problem!"

But think for a moment about the magnificent gift that God our Creator has given to us in the form of our bodies. All He asks is that we put the proper fuel into them and take care of them.

Paul urged, "I beseech you therefore, brethren, by the mercies of God, that you present your bodies a living sacrifice, holy, acceptable to God, which is your reasonable service" (Rom. 12:1). The Jews were big on sacrifice. They had an elaborate system for offering sheep, oxen, birds, and grain to God. Paul was saying to the Romans: Jesus has already paid the ultimate sacrifice for your sins. He asks only that you present your bodies as a *living* sacrifice to Him. Give Him your bodies to use. Allow Him to live out His life of ministry through your hands, your feet, your mouths, your minds, your actions.

Are you willing to present to God a cleaned-up body that's in good working order?

How many times do we find ourselves saying the following?

"I'm too tired to go to church for Bible study."

"I just don't have the energy to take on that ministry outreach."

"Let's go eat" as soon as the pastor says the final "amen" rather than spending time in prayer or lingering in fellowship with others in the church.

Presenting our bodies to the Lord means to be available and willing and ready for whatever task, opportunity, or challenge He puts in our paths.

We are to live balanced lives. God does not expect us to starve ourselves to death, just as He does not expect us to glut ourselves to death. We are to live healthy and balanced lives.

After I preached a sermon on nutrition one Sunday, I seemed to become Public Enemy Number One to all of the junk-food junkies in our church. Lisa and I were not invited to dinner for quite some time. People apparently concluded, "Ed drinks only carrot juice and eats only soy burgers." I watch what I eat, but I'm not a nut about it. I ask myself often, *Ed, are you glorifying God in your body? How are you treating the temple? What kind of fuel are you putting into the body God gave you?* We are to strive for balance.

We must get smart about what we eat. The Bible is filled with references to good, wholesome food. We find many references to whole grains, vegetables, and lean meats. Eating fruit is mentioned 200 times in the Bible. Drinking water is mentioned more than 350 times. Because Daniel ate vegetables and drank water, he won a physical-fitness contest over the Babylonians who ate sweet and fat "delicacies" and drank wine (see Dan. 1).

Eating right isn't enough. We must also be smart about exercise. Our bodies were created to move. But since most modern jobs don't involve physical labor, as work often did in the past, we have to find ways to give our bodies the exercise they need. We need to put on our jogging shoes—or our walking shoes—three to five times a week and get out there and move for thirty to forty-five minutes at a speed that gets our heart rate up to the proper levels.

Even more than diet and exercise, we are to have a right attitude in life. Proverbs 3:7–8 instructs us,

> Fear the LORD and depart from evil.
> It will be health to your flesh,
> And strength to your bones.

Getting the right foods and right exercise and right attitudes into *balance* is what God desires for us and expects of us.

Overcoming Gluttony Is a Gigantic Challenge

For those who struggle with it, gluttony is like a giant that looms in their path. It blocks out their hope of a future. It keeps them boxed in, hindered, and cowering.

That was the position the Israelites found themselves in. They were in a standoff with the Philistines, who had the best-trained army on earth. The Philistines had a corner on the iron market, which meant they had all of the war toys—all the chariots, swords, spears, and shields. In fact, the Philistines had so much "metal" power that if an Israelite needed to buy a pruning hook or have a plow sharpened, he had to consult a Philistine. By comparison, the Hebrews were a bunch of farmers and shepherds and fishermen who didn't know much about fighting.

Saul and his commander in chief, Abner, put together a group of volunteer soldiers to fight the Philistines, but the battle was at a stalemate. The Philistines were lined up on one hill, and the Israelites were on an opposite hill, with a little valley separating them.

David's brothers had gone off to be part of the army, and when the days turned to weeks, David's father, Jesse, sent David to take some food to his brothers on the front line. He didn't have to twist David's arm. David rushed to the front line, and when he got to the combat site, he was surprised. He didn't see what he had expected to see. Rather than a battle with spears flying, shields clanking, and people bleeding and dying, David found the armies sitting on their respective sides, hurling insults at each other. The soldiers were sitting around talking about their families and girlfriends and Saul's wealth. Nothing was happening.

David heard enough, however, to know that a guy who was about ten feet tall, with armor that weighed two hundred pounds, and a spear that weighed more than twenty-five pounds, had been daring the Israelites to fight him for weeks. This champion of the Philistines was the ultimate trash talker. He ridiculed the Israelites until they were scared to show their faces against the Philistines.

Gluttony can be that intimidating.

More than likely, you have heard someone say:

- "I've tried all of the diets. Not one works."
- "I've tried to resist desserts, but when chocolate shows up, my willpower walks out the door."
- "I've cut down on my drinking, but one or two glasses of wine at dinner aren't going to hurt me."

When gluttony has a hold on us, it has a hold primarily on our minds. We come to the place where we don't *think* we can overcome it. We get to the mental state where we don't even *care* that we don't think we can overcome it.

David had an opportunity to watch the Goliath show for himself. He saw a man who had graduated from war school. He had majored in assault and battery. He was mean as he taunted and cursed the Israelites and their God. He was the best of the Philistine best, which means in our terms that he was the baddest of the bad.

And David chose not to respond to this giant as every other Israelite on that hilltop had responded. He said, "I'll take him. God is with me."

That's precisely the point where a person must begin a battle against gluttony: "I'm going to lick this thing. God is with me."

You've got to settle the issue in your heart that you *are* going to overcome gluttony. And you must have an equal knowing that God is with you in your struggle, and He will help you.

Without resolve, you'll fall right back into the old pattern that has a hold on you. Without a sense that God is with you and is helping you, you'll attempt to overcome gluttony solely in your own strength, and you'll fail.

David's brothers quickly tried to keep David quiet. They said, "You just came down here to see us get killed. Who's watching the sheep anyway? Go back home where you belong!"

David didn't back down.

And neither should we when our friends come around saying such things as:

- "You don't really have a problem with this."
- "Everybody is a glutton at times—don't be so hard on yourself."

154

- "If you don't overindulge, people will think you're unappreciative, a party pooper, or self-righteous. Have a little fun!"

Ignore friends who try to dismiss the seriousness of gluttony. Gluttony is a fatal distraction. It is not to be taken lightly.

Soon, word reached King Saul that David was willing to fight. David said to Saul, "I'm willing to take this guy on." Saul tried to talk him out of the battle, but David pressed.

Then Saul did what many people do—he offered David a human solution. He lent David his armor. David put it on, and just as quickly, he took it off. He said, "This isn't for me."

Countless books on the market today tell us how to lose weight, improve our self-esteem, and overcome bad habits. Countless books are available to tell us how to simplify our lives and refrain from overindulgence. Nearly all of them present a human-only point of view. And that point of view will never succeed when it comes to slaying giants connected with fatal distractions.

We've got to keep in mind what the Philistines were after. They wanted the total surrender of the Israelites. They were after the Israelites to be their slaves, and slavery included serving the Philistine gods. David knew the battle was more than a physical fight. It was a spiritual battle, and it could be won only through total reliance upon the Lord.

The stakes for your life are the same. Satan isn't just after your body. He wants you to lose the battle against gluttony as a means of getting at your eternal soul. Various diet and fitness plans may help, but the definitive victory over gluttony must be won in the spirit realm.

When David walked out into the Valley of Elah, he walked alone, with only his staff in his hand and a sling and five smooth stones that he had pulled from the brook. Goliath had been ranting and raving and cursing for some time. When he saw David coming toward him, he laughed. "Hey, boy, what are you doing? Do you realize who you're fighting? I'll feed your flesh to the birds. You are coming to me with a stick. Am I a dog?"

David kept coming closer. And closer. And closer. The Bible says he ran toward Goliath. He began to twirl a stone around in his sling, and when he let it loose, that stone was traveling about two hundred feet a second so that it hit Goliath's head with about five thousand pounds of pressure per square inch—which is more powerful than a bullet from a Colt 45. The stone *sank* into Goliath's forehead, and he hit the deck, dust flying, armor clattering, and the rest of the Philistines freaking out. David finished off the job by pulling out Goliath's sword and cutting off Goliath's head with it.

Up on the hill, Saul rallied the troops, "Let's go get 'em, boys." The Israelites rushed into the valley and routed the Philistines, who turned and ran, leaving behind their artillery, their knapsacks, their money, and everything else of value. It was a great day for all of Israel, but especially a great day for David.

Using David's example, let me give you some tips on how to prepare to take out the giant of gluttony.

Prepare in Private

If you are going to take on a giant, prepare yourself. David had been working on his slingshot technique for years. That's what young shepherd boys did. They used their slingshots to scare away wild beasts. David got advanced training when his flock was attacked once by a lion and then another time by a bear.

Long before you go to the banquet, the feast, the festival, the party, the special event, or the restaurant, prepare yourself. Envision what you are likely to see and the wonderful aromas you are likely to smell, and then envision yourself saying, "No, thank you." Envision yourself putting only a small amount on your plate, and envision yourself being satisfied by it. Envision yourself declining the second helping. Envision yourself leaving a few bites of food on the plate.

Practice in the privacy of your own home. Eat only until you are full. That takes practice! It takes discipline and restraint to reach the point where you can say "enough" when you are full. It takes patience to eat slowly enough so the message can get from the stomach to the brain that you are full.

Part of your practice should be prayer. Matthew 14:23 gives us a critical insight into the ministry of

Jesus: Jesus "went up on the mountain by Himself to pray." Tell God about your problem with overindulgence and excess. Admit it to yourself and to Him. And then ask for His help.

Fight the Right Foe

The problem with gluttony is in your attitude toward food and drink, and toward your body. The problem is not with those who are good cooks, with a mother or spouse who puts before you the "wrong foods," with the menu in the cafeteria at work, with the TV commercial producers, or with the genetic background you inherited from your parents. The problem lies in your willpower.

Many people get so angry and upset with other people, and even with themselves, that they fail to focus on the real issue: their inability to say yes and no at the right times.

Focus on yes and no. Focus on what it means for you to take control over your fleshly desires rather than have them take control over you. Focus on each opportunity to say no. Count it as an opportunity to grow in spiritual strength.

David did not allow any of his disgust and anger at Goliath to be siphoned off and used against his brother Eliab or others who ridiculed him. He stayed focused on the real enemy, the giant down in the valley.

Don't fight the wrong enemies. Don't lash out at other people for not helping you more or for tempting you with hot-fudge sundaes. Don't put the blame on others. Face up to the real enemy—the one associated with your willpower.

Develop Your Own Strategy for Increasing Your Willpower

Developing willpower is important in dealing with all of the fatal distractions, but perhaps most of all in dealing with the sin of gluttony.

People often say, "I just don't have any willpower." The fact is, you do. You have been given a measure of willpower by God. You have been given the free *will* to make choices. You have been given the *power* of the Holy Spirit in your life. Your free *will* plus the Holy Spirit's *power* gives you *willpower*!

Rather than deny, diminish, or downplay your willpower, choose to develop it.

How? By doing the things that you know are good for the spirit.

Spend time with God, talking to Him and listening to Him.

Read the Scriptures daily, perhaps even several times a day for a few minutes each time. Select Bible verses so that you always are in the process of memorizing a particular verse that is helpful to you in your struggle against gluttony.

Attend church regularly, and become involved in some form of ministry. Be faithful in your attendance, your giving, your involvement, your commitments.

The more you discipline yourself in these areas that build up the spirit, the stronger you are going to grow in willpower. It is then a matter of turning your laser-beam, highly honed willpower toward the temptation of gluttony.

The exact plan for developing your willpower should

be *your* plan. Not every person is going to be inspired by the same Bible verses or feel drawn to the same types of ministry. Part of developing willpower is developing what fits *you*. Ask the Lord to show you the optimal, just-for-you plan to fight gluttony.

Notice the progression in David's preparation for battle: "He took his staff in his hand; and he chose for himself five smooth stones from the brook, and put them in a shepherd's bag, in a pouch which he had, and his sling was in his hand" (1 Sam. 17:40). David wasn't without armor—it just wasn't the kind of armor that King Saul wore.

The Bible tells us that Saul stood head and shoulders over all the other Israelites—he probably wore a fifty-eight long. There was no way David was going to be comfortable in Saul's gear. Neither are you likely to be comfortable in following somebody else's disciplinary pattern when it comes to willpower. Develop what fits you.

Value Your Victories

Trophies remind us of our victories. Most people love receiving them. The trophy may not be the kind that is placed on the mantel in the family room. It may be an honor or reward of another kind, perhaps even one that is intangible. The main benefit of trophies, rewards, and honors is that they evoke the memory of our victories—the times when we truly were winners.

David certainly valued his victory over Goliath. He

took Goliath's head back to Jerusalem, and he put Goliath's armor in his tent. Goliath's head was a sign to all of Israel that they were free from the giant Philistine. The armor was a private sign to David that great things are possible when a man trusts God.

I encourage you to keep a prayer journal. Write out your prayers. And in your journal, keep track of your victories. Record how and when God answers your prayers. Over time, your prayer journal will be a source of inspiration to you—you will begin to see a pattern of how God has helped you through one victory after another.

No victory is too small to record. If the victory was simply saying no to a second teaspoon of dressing on your salad, record it! When you feel that you are a failure and that you will never conquer gluttony, take out your prayer journal and read it. See how God has been faithful to you in the past when you have placed your trust in Him.

Other tangible things are good for you to have around, at least for a while, to remind you of God's faithfulness in helping you overcome your battle against temptation. Such a reminder might be a set of before-and-after photos or a pair of pants that has become too big for you. Count these things as faith trophies.

Anticipate the Giant's Return

Most people try to live Goliath-free lives. We like to think, *Well, I've defeated that sin. I'll never have to fight that battle again.*

The reality is that we never entirely get away from giants. Nobody lives a trouble-free life, no matter how his life may appear on the surface. David never had to fight the champion of the Philistines again, but he did have to fight Philistines again. You are likely to have a battle with gluttony all your life, to lesser or greater degrees. Choose to engage in the war against gluttony for the long haul. Every day may not be a battle—every meal may not be a temptation, every party may not be a war zone—but be ready for battle when battle times come.

How do you remain alert and ready?

An effective tool for maintaining victory in this area is to fast and pray from time to time. Choose to skip a meal and to spend that time in prayer about a specific issue, problem, or circumstance that is troubling you.

Be constant in the disciplines that strengthen your spirit—the same disciplines discussed earlier in the context of developing willpower. Stay true to what you know will keep you strong in the Lord.

And finally, be alert to times when you know gluttony is likely to rear its gigantic head. For most of us, one of those times is likely to be Thanksgiving dinner. It may be the holiday season as a whole, from Thanksgiving all the way to New Year's Day. It may be vacation time. It may be a specific party or celebration. Anticipate in advance that gluttony is likely to be lurking in the shadows of any event that offers fun, festivity, and food.

COUNT THE TOTAL COST

One of the best pieces of advice about gluttony is found in Proverbs 23:1–3:

> When you sit down to eat with a ruler,
> Consider carefully what is before you;
> And put a knife to your throat
> If you are a man given to appetite.
> Do not desire his delicacies,
> For they are deceptive food.

Solomon wasn't referring literally to slitting one's throat at a king's banquet table. He was saying that there's a price to pay for everything you take into your life. Weigh the total cost of what you consume.

Is it worth being disobedient to God?

Is it worth becoming distracted from all God has for you?

Is it worth falling short of what you might accomplish for the Lord in your lifetime?

Make your answer no to each of these questions!

Gluttony is a giant that can be conquered. Take courage and engage in the battle.

8

GREED

Rewiring the Desire to Acquire Gone Haywire

One of my favorite sports is professional wrestling. I use the word *sport* loosely, of course. Much of the wrestling that appears on television is not Olympic-quality athleticism. It's fake, it's phony, and it's fun to watch.

Through the years, I've seen some of the best: Chief Wahoo McDaniel, Fritz von Eric, the Missing Link, Andre the Giant, and Hulk Hogan. Undoubtedly my favorite wrestler, however, was the man often introduced as the "big blond bruiser from Abilene, Texas, Dusty Rhodes—the American Dream!"

Every wrestler seems to have his favorite hold, and Dusty's hold was one he called the sleeper. He would grab his opponent's neck and head from behind and begin to squeeze. Opponents rarely had a chance. They eventually had to submit to the sleeper. Dusty frequently appeared prior to his matches, saying, "Let me tell you somethin'— I'm 287 pounds of sweet soul, and once I put the sleeper on your big ol' head, it's over, Jack." Nine times out of ten he was right.

Most Christians I know today are in a hold. It is a grip that is real, severe, and deadly. It is the grip of greed.

Greed is a sin that we always see in other people, but we rarely see in ourselves. Just at the mention of the word *greed,* a picture of a person probably popped into your mind— but that person probably wasn't you. Sometimes the greedy person we envision is a spouse, whom we wish would guard the charge cards a little more closely. Sometimes it's a friend. Sometimes it's someone we observe from afar. Our entire society seems caught in the grip of this fatal distraction. We all seem to have been weaned on want. We feed on greed—more so than any other generation in the history of our nation and perhaps even the world.

Greed says, "I want more than my life's share of goodies." It always holds out an unkeepable promise that it can be satisfied: "Just a little more and then I'll stop." But a little more never satisfies. There's always one more deal, one more transaction, one more check, one more car, one more house, one more suit, one more belt, one more dress, one more boat, one more jet ski, one more rod and reel. Just one more.

Greed-focused and greed-empowered messages bombard us. Advertisers are paid billions of dollars every year to brainwash us with unique combinations of sights, sounds, and messages to convince us that we *need* particular products to the point that we cannot resist buying them. In reality, we rarely need what advertisers offer us.

I define *greed* as "the desire to acquire gone haywire."

The Bible has numerous examples of this sin in action.

Greed caused Eve to desire and acquire forbidden fruit.

Greed fueled Lot's desire to take the plain of Jordan.

Greed caused Samuel's sons to take under-the-table bribes.

Greed led Esau to sell his birthright and blessing to Jacob.

Greed caused the rich young ruler to turn away from following Jesus.

Greed caused a wealthy man to miss out on paradise, while a man named Lazarus attained it.

Greed motivated the money changers to set up their tables in the temple.

Greed was at the heart of Judas's betrayal of Jesus.

WHAT WOULD YOU DO FOR $10 MILLION?

In the best-selling book *The Day America Told the Truth,* the results of a number of surveys were reported.

One of them dealt with answers to the question, "How far would you go for $10 million?"

Twenty-five percent of Americans said they would be willing to abandon all of their friends. Twenty-three percent said they would be willing to work as a prostitute for a week. Sixteen percent would give up their citizenship. Ten percent said they would withhold testimony that would allow a murderer to go free. Seven percent would murder a stranger. Six percent would change their race. And four percent would have a sex-change operation.

Even children's books recognize the deadly grip of greed. Stan and Jan Berenstain, whose book series about the Berenstain Bears has sold millions of copies, have a book about a brother and sister bear who become infected with the "Galloping Greedy Gimmies." I have read this book to my four children more times than I can count. It packs a potent message about what can happen when greed takes over our lives.

WHICH TYPE OF GETTER ARE YOU?

There seem to be two general types of getters:

1. Velcro Getters

These people receive from God, and everything they receive sticks to them. Our twins for a while had an almost automatic response anytime I touched one of their toys. They'd say, "It's not yours!" They were acting like Velcro getters.

2. Teflon Getters

These people receive from God, and what they receive slides right off of them to bless others. They don't hoard. They don't stockpile. They don't have vast resources set aside for a rainy day that never comes. They receive from God and they pass it on.

Certainly I am not opposed to people having savings accounts or making sound, long-term investments. What I oppose, and what I believe the Word of God opposes, is the habit of believing that we never have enough; therefore, we keep everything we receive and grasp for more.

Greed says to God and to others about the things that are acquired, "It's not yours!" Greed says to God, "I don't trust You to meet my needs. I don't trust You to replace what I give with even more of what I need." Greed puts reliance upon the acquisition and possession of things more than upon trust in God. And that is *precisely* why greed is a fatal distraction.

Proverbs 11:24–26 comments on givers and getters:

There is one who scatters, yet increases more;
And there is one who withholds more than is right,
But it leads to poverty.
The generous soul will be made rich,
And he who waters will also be watered himself.

The people will curse him who withholds grain,
But blessing will be on the head of him who sells it.

Velcro getters are people who will be cursed for with-
holding what they could have given to help others. Teflon
getters are those who will be blessed for giving.

GREED VS. AMBITION

In times past, greed was openly talked about as a
vice. But in many circles, it is now paraded as a virtue,
a sign of having a competitive edge, being ambitious and
a go-getter.

Many people actually seem to believe that greed is
good. It is a sign of being highly motivated toward success. It is a sign of people who like nice things. Of course,
those who hold such a high opinion of greed rarely call it
greed. Rather, they call it a desire to improve oneself, a
desire to reach the top, a desire to set goals and reach
them, or a desire to have nice things. It is associated with
having good taste—it is first cousin to style, gourmet
tastes, and an appreciation for quality. It is the motivation that leads people to never settle for second best.

If we do admit that greed is wrong, we certainly don't
believe it is a serious sin. We think of greed as a rather
minor problem that can be dealt with easily. We don't
consider it to be a *deadly* sin.

Throughout the Bible, however, we find a number of lists of wicked behaviors, which some people call vice lists. And nearly always, greed is included on the list. It is found alongside such nasty behaviors as murder, deceit, sexual immorality, idolatry, and drunkenness. The Bible calls greed a "grievous" sin. Rather than go gaga over the manifestations of greed, we should say, "Aaagggh!"

GOD'S REMEDY FOR GREED

The Bible presents only one behavior and attitude that can break the grip of greed: generosity. The Bible challenges us to get out of our comfort zone and start giving generously. Giving isn't a nice suggestion in the Bible. It is a commandment. Generous giving is the exact opposite of greedy grasping.

Greed is self-centered and selfish. Generosity is other-focused and selfless.

Greed hoards. Generosity relinquishes.

Greed holds a tight grip. Generosity shares freely.

Greed is closefisted. Generosity is openhanded, with arms spread wide to embrace problems and people who have problems.

Greed keeps mental lists of wants. Generosity keeps mental lists of people and projects that need assistance.

The apostle Paul taught these major points about generosity:

Generosity in Attitude

Paul taught that we are to have an attitude of joy when we give: "So let each one give as he purposes in his heart, not grudgingly or of necessity; for God loves a cheerful giver" (2 Cor. 9:7). The word *cheerful* in this passage literally means "with hilarity." We are to be hilarious givers! We are to be excited about giving, eager to give, and bring our offerings laughing all the way.

I have never met a negative generous person. Generous people are usually upbeat, positive, optimistic, and faith-filled.

Giving with a cheerful heart also means that we give without an ulterior motive. Generosity is not a gimmick. It is giving without any strings attached. How many people do we know who give, but their real intent is to get something back? They have one hand out to give, but the other hand is poised and ready to receive.

God never promises us that we are going to receive from the person to whom we give. Nor does He promise us that we are going to receive something immediately.

A person can take one of two attitudes toward giving. He can regard it as something he *has* to do, or he can regard it as something he *gets* to do.

Those who regard giving as something they have to do tend to believe that they earned what they have. I have overheard people say, "I spent long, hard hours earning my money, and then the church just wants to take it away." They do *not* have a cheerful heart about giving. They are giving grudgingly.

If you have the attitude that you were solely responsible for earning what you have, and therefore it is yours to do with as you please, let me share this reality shocker with you: *You did not earn what you have without God's help.* He gives you the talent and ability you have. He gives you every breath of your lungs and every beat of your heart. He gives you energy and strength to work hard. He has given you the ability to think new thoughts, make new plans, dream new dreams, set new goals, invent new products, come up with new services, and develop new strategies. You wouldn't have anything if God didn't give it to you first.

The Bible explains that God gives seed to the sower and bread to the eater (Isa. 55:10). He gives opportunity. He puts people in the right place at the right time. There are no coincidences in God's plan.

The person who believes that all he has is a gift from God is much more likely to have a cheerful attitude toward giving and to give generously.

And what does God require of us? An older shopkeeper once noted, "I like doing business with God. He requires all of my heart but only 10 percent of my income." God has set the standard of the tithe for our giving—the *tithe* literally means "ten." We are to give a tenth of our income to the Lord's work. But what we give in offerings is totally up to us. Paul said, "Let each one give as he purposes in his heart" (2 Cor. 9:7). "As he purposes" means "as he decides." Your total giving is an act of your will.

Generous giving always starts with a generous attitude.

Generosity in Action

Have you ever heard someone say, "Well, someday if I have the money, I'd like to . . ."? And then he identifies a particular charity he'd like to help. Most people are generous in their talk, but not in their deeds.

God calls us to be generous right where we are with what we presently have.

Now there are those who are unwise in what they give. They give to strangers and to faraway causes while they let their families go hungry or their churches shrivel. They give rather than pay their bills. They go into debt to make a show of their giving. That's not only bad stewardship; it's an act of pride.

Where is the balance between generosity and responsibility?

We are to give with a generous heart to the point that our giving involves self-sacrifice. We are not to sacrifice the welfare of others. We are not to give more than we have; rather, we are to give a significant percentage of what we have to the point that we willingly and freely give up personal luxuries to help those who don't have the basics.

Generosity in Harvest

Paul declared, "He who sows sparingly will also reap sparingly, and he who sows bountifully will also reap bountifully" (2 Cor. 9:6). Those of us who are city slickers may have a tough time comprehending this agricultural verse. The point is, skimpy seed sowing, skimpy harvest; generous seed sowing, generous harvest.

Giving and receiving are in a proportionate cycle. That cycle is expected to go round and round, with greater and greater generosity and bigger and bigger harvests. We are privileged to give, and when we give with a generous attitude, we will be blessed by what God gives back to us.

God issued a giving challenge to His people. The Israelites at the time were not bringing their offerings to the temple in Jerusalem as God had commanded. The Lord spoke to them through the prophet Malachi:

> "Will a man rob God?
> Yet you have robbed Me!
> But you say,
> 'In what way have we robbed You?'
> In tithes and offerings.
> You are cursed with a curse,
> For you have robbed Me,
> Even this whole nation.
> Bring all the tithes into the storehouse,
> That there may be food in My house,
> And try Me now in this,"
> Says the LORD of hosts,
> "If I will not open for you the windows of heaven
> And pour out for you such blessing
> That there will not be room enough to receive it."
> (Mal. 3:8–10)

The Lord promised the Israelites a blessing that would be too great to contain! I don't know about you, but that's the kind of blessing I want.

Are you willing to take God's challenge to "prove Him"?

I know several people who are being blessed financially but aren't all that smart. They'd be the first to say, "I'm not all that great. Why am I making so much money?" I believe the reason for their financial blessing is their generosity. God trusts them and their families to recycle the blessing they receive, so the gospel can be spread in new and innovative ways and the kingdom of God can be advanced.

Paul LeTourneau is often remembered for the college he founded and funded, LeTourneau University. But Paul LeTourneau had an even greater legacy. He was a consummate, world-class giver. From the time he was a young man, he gave tithes and generous offerings to God's work. Giving became the pattern of his life. It was his habit to be generous.

The more he gave, the more prosperous he became. God didn't rain hundred-dollar bills down from heaven. But God gave him great ideas about the creation of new products. The more successful the products were in meeting needs, the greater the income to LeTourneau, the greater the amount of his tithes, and the greater his percentage of offerings.

In the beginning, LeTourneau gave 10 percent of a very small amount. At the end of his life, he was giving God 90 percent of a very large amount. Who benefited? Everybody! The 10 percent LeTourneau kept for himself at the end of his life was a far greater amount than the 90 percent he had kept as a young man.

LeTourneau didn't go from giving God 10 percent to giving God 90 percent overnight. The process was gradual and steady. The more LeTourneau gave, the more he received, the more he gave, the more he received, and the more he gave. That's God's plan, not just for Paul LeTourneau, but for all Christians who will take God's dare in "proving Him" with their giving.

How Do You Feel About Giving to Your Church?

Do you have a generous attitude when it comes to giving to your church? Or do you resent what you give to the church?

I refuse to feel embarrassed when it comes to talking about money. Some people complain that preachers spend too much time talking about money, but let me tell you, those who complain usually need to hear the message the most. The generous person doesn't get upset when a sermon is about money. The stingy person, who trusts in his own wealth and who doesn't want to part with any of it for the gospel's sake, gets upset when a sermon is about money.

Are you aware that one out of ten verses in the Gospels deals with money and material wealth? Sixteen out of Jesus' thirty-eight parables deal with money and possessions. There are about five hundred verses in the Bible about prayer, and about five hundred more about faith, but twenty-three hundred verses are on the wise use of money and possessions. God desires for us to be generous with the material wealth He gives us. He wants us to know how to use money in right ways.

The result of generous giving to God's work is the salvation of souls. Generous giving also results in spiritual growth for believers. If you want spiritual prosperity, give generously. If you want spiritual decay and decline, give in to greed.

GENEROSITY ISN'T ONLY A MATTER OF MONEY

Generosity is often thought of in terms of money—just as greed is often viewed in terms of money and possessions—but generosity is an attitude of the heart. It goes far beyond the wallet.

Generosity is expressed when we take extra time with a person:

- We listen with even more compassion and intensity.

- We go out of our way to make someone else's day.

- We volunteer to do the chore that we least like and that really isn't our assigned chore.

The rewards from generosity are not limited to money either. Generosity is a key to moving our relationships to the next level. It is the key to opening up our minds to new possibilities and opportunities. It is the key to experiencing love.

When we are generous, we encourage generosity in others. We stir up others to get out of themselves and to do things pleasing to God. Paul wrote to the Corinthians,

> Now concerning the ministering to the saints . . . I know your willingness [which has also been translated "enthusiasm"], about which I boast of you to the Macedonians . . . and your zeal has stirred up the majority. (2 Cor. 9:1–2)

The generosity of the Corinthians had wide-reaching effects. Their giving fired up others to give. Not everybody was stirred—there always seems to be a miser in every group—but Paul said the majority was stirred. What a great reputation to have—a giver who inspires others to give!

Who would you rather be around? A stingy person or a generous person? I don't know of anybody who enjoys the company of a stingy person. Generous people attract friends and keep friends. They have a good reputation. They are joys to have in any group. They make the best spouses. They are a pastor's delight.

And for whom are you likely to go a second mile—a stingy person or a generous person? The generous person, of course. A generous person is most likely to receive the most help when he is in need.

We Grow in Grace

Yet another benefit of generosity is that our giving helps us grow in grace. The generous person has a greater understanding about how God works and about what God asks of us and has done for us. Was Jesus a generous person? He was *the* most generous person who ever lived! He gave all that He had so that others might benefit, even to the point of giving His life on the cross.

Our Souls Are Knit to Others'

When we are generous toward others—when we give to others, when we help others—our souls are knit to their souls. We feel greater compassion for them. We have greater concern for their concerns. We remember to pray more often for them.

We Are More Effective Witnesses

Paul said about the Corinthians, "They glorify God for the obedience of your confession to the gospel of Christ, and for your liberal sharing" (2 Cor. 9:13). A hallmark of any Christian is that he is a good example of God at work in his life.

The members of my church congregation are a tremendous inspiration to me in the way they give. Their giving and their generous spirit attract those who don't know the Lord. Their example is talked about all over the area where we live and worship. They have developed a reputation as an alive, active, caring group of people.

Their generosity is a powerful agent in causing souls to be saved and lives to be turned around.

We are all being watched by somebody. The world at large is not generous—it is focused on acquiring, not giving. When the world sees people giving, it takes notice. It looks more closely. When it sees those people giving cheerfully, it looks even more closely. When it sees and hears about the love of God that motivates the people to give, it looks closer still. Step-by-step, those who watch generous givers are drawn closer and closer to Jesus Christ. That's what generosity is all about. It's about getting beyond ourselves, so we can impact others for Christ.

Can you see why greed is so deadly? It not only kills something inside us, it has a deadly effect on the body of Christ.

FOUR MANEUVERS TO STAY OUT OF THE GRIP OF GREED

When it comes to a fatal distraction, the best move to make is to turn away from the possibility of sinning before the opportunity arises. This especially is true for greed. Four maneuvers can help you stay out of the grip of greed.

1. Learn the Secret of Admiring Only

Learn the secret of admiring without desiring. If you can look at something and admire it without feeling that you have to own it personally, you will save yourself thousands upon thousands of dollars. Develop the ability to look at something in a store window and say, "Wow, that's really awesome," but don't say, "That's really awesome, so I've got to own it." What you don't own:

- You don't have to dust or clean.
- You don't have to insure.
- You don't have to paint, shine, or polish.
- You don't have to maintain.

Refuse to allow goods to become gods.

No person can be obsessed with God and goods at the same time. Jesus taught, "Take heed and beware of covetousness, for one's life does not consist in the abundance of the things he possesses" (Luke 12:15).

2. Learn the Secret of Giving Stuff Away

Is there something in your life that you are clinging to? Is there something you desperately don't want to lose, part with, or leave behind when you die?

About once every three months I try to give away something that I truly value. No strings attached. No giving the item to my wife so it will stay in the family. I just give it away. What does this do for me? It helps me to stay free of greed and to put things into their proper perspective.

We are to love people and use things to show love to

people. Greed sets in when we start to love things and use people to get things.

3. Learn the Secret of Being Generous Toward God

The Jews hated Zacchaeus because he was a tax collector for Rome. Tax collectors were notorious for overcharging whenever they could get away with it. Some of them managed to become very wealthy because they passed on very little of what they collected to the Jews. In other words, they were rip-off artists. Zacchaeus was that type of person.

Jesus invited Zacchaeus to a power luncheon at Zacchaeus's house. While He was there, Zacchaeus said, "Lord, I give half of my goods to the poor; and if I have taken anything from anyone by false accusation, I restore fourfold" (Luke 19:8). Jesus replied, "Today salvation has come to this house" (v. 9).

Jesus did not mean that Zacchaeus's soul was saved because he gave away money. He meant that Zacchaeus was on the road to getting things right with other people and with God because he had repented of his greed and was making a move toward generosity. Sometimes the best way for us to grow in our relationship with God and other people is to give up something we value highly.

Are you content with your contents? Contentment is not a lack of ambition or drive. It is not being lethargic or lazy. Contentment develops in us when we are free of being overly concerned and preoccupied with things. When things lose their hold on us, we truly are free.

One day a young man came to Jesus and said, "My father died and my brother has taken all of the inheritance for himself. Tell my brother to divide the inheritance with me." Jesus said, "One's life does not consist in the abundance of the things he possesses" (Luke 12:15). But Jesus didn't leave the matter there. He went on to tell a story:

> The ground of a certain rich man yielded plentifully. And he thought within himself, saying, "What shall I do, since I have no room to store my crops?" So he said, "I will do this: I will pull down my barns and build greater, and there I will store all my crops and my goods. And I will say to my soul, 'Soul, you have many goods laid up for many years; take your ease; eat, drink, and be merry.'" But God said to him, "Fool! This night your soul will be required of you; then whose will those things be which you have provided?" (vv. 16–20)

Jesus ended the story by saying, "So is he who lays up treasure for himself, and is not rich toward God" (Luke 12:21).

Some of the wealthiest people I know are bankrupt in relationships, including their relationship with God. Money cannot buy eternal happiness or the genuine riches of the heart. Eternal *life* is the product of faith; eternal *rewards* are the product of generosity.

4. Learn the Reality of Death and Its Relationship to Things
Death marks the final failure of things. We might flash

our cash on this earth, but we cannot take anything with us when we die.

My father-in-law died recently. I have known him most of my life and have admired him greatly. He was one of the best fathers on this earth. The hardest public speaking challenge I have ever faced was to preach his funeral—it was impossible to summarize the goodness and the spiritual magnitude of this man in a few words and a few minutes.

As I reflected on Mendel's life, I came again and again to the word *generous*. For example, if Mendel came across a family stranded alongside a freeway, he not only stopped to see what he could do to help them, he also offered them the use of his car!

Mendel had a neighbor who was a crusty old miser. This man ridiculed Mendel for his faith, but one day just a couple of months before Mendel died, he had the opportunity to lead this neighbor to a personal relationship with Christ. Mendel had been generous over the years in his prayers for this man and in his kindness to him.

There was also the time when Mendel and his wife, Elva, took in a young couple who needed a home. The young man was a golf pro, and he and his girlfriend had just accepted Christ but were living in sexual sin. Mendel and Elva gave them a home and discipled them in the Lord and then paid for their wedding! Mendel gave away the bride at the ceremony. Another time, they gave a man who had lost his job a home for four months, rent free.

Mendel was not a rich man. He was a retired postal

worker who did a little landscape work on the side. But every week, Mendel wrote out a generous check to his church. As I was looking through his ledger, I also saw entry after entry of checks written to the church I pastor. I was amazed. I had no idea Mendel had given so much to the work of the Lord. His giving was quiet, constant, and generous—again and again and again.

ASK GOD TO ENLARGE YOUR HEART

In a tag-team wrestling match, one of the two team members might be caught in a powerful hold, but if he can move just a few inches and touch the fingertips of his teammate outside the ring, that teammate can jump over the ropes and save the day.

That's the hope we have if we find we are caught in the grip of greed. Our loving God is just beyond the edge of the ring. If we will reach out to Him and ask Him to free us from the hold that things have on our lives, He will free us from greed.

Many of us pray often for God to enlarge our income, enlarge our houses, enlarge our influence, enlarge our families, enlarge our companies, enlarge our bank accounts, enlarge our investment portfolios. Choose today to ask God to enlarge your heart to give.

Ask Him to rewire in you any desire to acquire that has gone haywire.

9
LIFE-ENRICHING ATTRACTIONS

The Costs and Benefits of Growing Up Spiritually

Every year I was in junior high school, the administration divided the boys and girls into two large groups, and each group saw a sex education film. I never saw the girls' video, *From Girl to Woman*, but I did see the guys' video, *From Boy to Man*. The film made an indelible impression on my life.

The actor was a pubescent youngster named Jim. The film showed Jim playing basketball. He was a horrible player. He dressed about fifteen years out of style. He wore a plaid short-sleeved shirt, rolled-up Levi's, and black PF Flyer tennis shoes. The announcer would describe Jim: "Look at Jim. He is growing up now. See the muscularity; see the coordination. Notice Jim's voice is changing." Jim would shout, "Pass me the ball," and his voice would break in the middle of the sentence.

Then the cruel, sadistic announcer would say, "Jim is also becoming interested in girls. Let's listen in." Jim would put the basketball down and walk into his house, open up the fridge, get a big cold glass of milk, walk to the telephone, wipe the perspiration from his brow, and dial. "May I speak to Sally, please. Sally, this is Jim. I am in your science class. I was wondering if you would like to go to the dance with me this Friday night. You would? Neato. That is great. Bye."

Then Jim would place his hands behind his neck and lean back. The announcer would say, "Look at Jim's armpits. Notice the rings of perspiration. See the peach fuzz on his chin. Jim is going through puberty. He is moving from boy to man." Then the music would start. "This is the documentary that will teach you about human development."

Every year it was the same old drill in the same old classroom with the same old film about the same old Jim.

The guy never matured! He stayed stuck in puberty. If the film was made today, Jim would be wearing a Tommy Hilfiger outfit, he might have a nose ring, and he'd have a boom box blaring at his side while he shot hoops, but he'd still be Jim.

That's where a lot of Christians are. They are stuck in spiritual adolescence. They're still dealing with the same ol' adolescent patterns.

THE TELLTALE MARKS OF
SPIRITUAL ADOLESCENCE

We need to grow out of several characteristics of spiritual adolescence.

Autonomy

Adolescents love to flex their autonomy. They want to prove they can go it alone. They see themselves as the center of their universe. No one can tell them what to do— not a parent, not a teacher, not a politician, not a coach, and especially not a pastor. They cut themselves off from the advice of mature adults.

Don't fall into that trap. Autonomy is another name for pride.

God calls us to submit our autonomy to His authority. God gives us a flow chart, a chain of command. He puts people and institutions over us, and as a result, we learn to submit to authority. As we mature, He puts people under us, and as a result, we learn to serve. At all times, He tells us we are part of the family of God.

Whether we're in a company or on a team or in a church, we are to be in relationship with other people. We submit to some in that group because they are in authority. We lead and mentor and teach and serve others in the group because we are in authority over them.

That's God's plan. We have no autonomy. We don't live life alone. We are welded to other people.

Rule-Testing

Adolescents test the rules.

When I was fifteen years old, I got a permanent driver's license. You could get a license at fifteen in South Carolina, but it was a restricted license. By law, I had to be in by eight o'clock at night.

I asked my parents if I could use the car one Wednesday night to take Lisa to a midweek service. They allowed me to use the car, but they reminded me that Lisa lived sixteen miles away and the law said I had to be home by eight o'clock. My father said, "Son, be in by eight. We are going to trust you." It was my first time to drive their car alone.

I couldn't wait for church to get out. The service ended about 6:30 P.M., and Lisa and I hopped in the station wagon and drove to her house. I thought to myself, *This will be the night I'll kiss Lisa for the first time.* I had on my Jovan musk oil.

We sat in her driveway for a while as I got up enough courage to kiss her. I looked at my watch, and suddenly it was 7:55 P.M.! My home was sixteen miles away, but I didn't worry about that. I finally kissed her about 8:05—it was a magical moment. The next thing I remember, I looked at my watch, and it was 8:20. I told Lisa I had to go. I was breaking the law and breaking my parents' rule. I walked her to the door, gave her another quick kiss, jumped back into my mom's station wagon, and was glad it had a 455 under the hood. I flew home.

I wasn't all that worried because Dad was a pastor, and

it was Wednesday night, so I figured he'd have meetings scheduled after church. I knew I could talk my way past my sweet, gentle, nice mom. I also knew the speed limit was fifty-five, but I went eighty-five. I careened into my neighborhood, and I passed a car that looked amazingly like my father's car. I reassured myself that was impossible. My father never came directly home from church, but just in case, I said a quick prayer that the car was *not* my father's.

I pulled into the driveway and was ecstatic that my father's car wasn't there. I bounded into the kitchen and apologized to my mother for being late. She said in her Mississippi accent, "Ed, where have you been? We have been worried about you." I said, "Mom, I'm sorry I'm late. Dad had a meeting at church, right?" She said, "Ed, he is out looking for you."

I'll never forget the moment. I turned and saw the headlights reflect on the pine trees as my father's car came screaming up the driveway. Then in kind of a Starsky and Hutch power turn, he stopped the car, got out, and said to me, "Keys. Driver's license." I took out my wallet to find my license, and he told me to give him the whole wallet.

He said, "Edwin Barry Young, you disobeyed me. You disobeyed the law. You disobeyed your mom. Your summer, Ed, is mine. For the next two weeks you will be out front in our flower bed and you will be pulling nut grass from sunup to sundown. Nut grass. By yourself."

That flower bed—which was really a weed bed—was

about double the size of the stage of our church. It was monstrous.

Our heavenly Father tells us we have to be in by eight. But we reply, "I've got the keys and a girl. I'll do what I please, thank You very much." And some of us find ourselves reaping the consequences, pulling nut grass in the hot summer sun.

Are you still testing God's rules?

Fads

Adolescents are into fads. They are always changing fashions, clichés, music. Recently I was in a store shopping for a swimsuit. I saw a seventeen-year-old guy standing near me, and I pulled out a pair of trunks and asked his opinion. He said, "Nah, man, those were in six months ago, but they're not anymore." He chose other swim trunks and assured me they *were* cool. He said I could boogie board with 'em, surf with 'em, and fish with 'em. He sold me.

A lot of people approach church with a fad mind-set. They move from church to church, from fad to fad, from fashion to fashion, from teacher to teacher. They never land. And that means they never put down roots to grow. They never really become involved so they can learn how to love. They never build, so they have no commitment to what is built. And they remain camped on the plains of puberty.

Each one of the seven fatal distractions is subject to a fad way of thinking. The "in" food, restaurant, or beverage today isn't "in" next month. Excuses for pride come and go. We lust after one movie star today and another next week.

The things of God are lasting. His love is classic. His trustworthiness is rock solid. His desire to forgive never wavers.

Aren't you ready to grow up and invest in things that really count and really last—I mean *really* last—for all eternity?

Come-and-Go Interests

Adolescents live in the moment. The crisis of today is rarely the crisis of tomorrow. Boyfriends can change hourly. Hairstyles rarely last an entire day.

An adolescent's life can seem like a puzzle with lots of moving parts. There's very little focus.

I hate ruts. I'm all for breaking out of them.

I like new things. I like change.

But I've also come to know that some things should never change. God's central place in our lives is one of them.

When I look at the way a lot of people live, I see gumbo. Gumbo has lots of ingredients. So do their lives. They have a fast-track career, soccer star kids, and a golf score in the low eighties. They have read the latest novel, seen the latest movie, and run the latest 10K race. And they have just enough room to add a little God to the gumbo of their lives. They stir God in as if He is just one more ingredient in the recipe.

God is not some insignificant tag on to our lives. He is not seasoning. God wants to wear the chef's hat. He wants to put the recipe together. He wants to tell us our spiritual, relational, emotional, biological, and psychological priorities.

A spiritually mature person puts God at the controls of his life and keeps Him there.

THE COSTS OF SPIRITUAL MATURITY

Growing up spiritually involves big costs:

A Relational Cost

The Bible says that we, as Christians, are *not* to be joined to nonbelievers: "Do not be unequally yoked together with unbelievers" (2 Cor. 6:14). That's a popular verse for married Christians but not a popular verse for those who are dating. That one verse eliminates about four-fifths of all potential dating candidates. The verse isn't limited to dating, however. It applies to any people with whom we might choose to be in a contractual agreement.

That verse does not mean that we are to become bigots or racists. Don't think for one minute that God is involved in spiritual apartheid. If we aren't involved with other people, how can they know about God? How can they see that God makes a difference in a person's life? We are to be involved in the lives of people outside the family of God. We aren't to enter into just any type of binding agreement with them. Our closest companions are to be those who share the common denominator of Christ.

For many people, the price of limiting close friendships, dating relationships, and contractual relationships to Christians is a high price to pay. But it's a requirement for spiritual maturity.

A Time Cost

If we really want to grow spiritually, we are going to have to feed on God's Word, learn how to talk to God in prayer, and understand how to walk in fellowship with other believers. Doing these things takes a lot of discretionary time. We won't have the same amount of time in our schedules for "hanging out." Blocks of time are required if we are to develop communion with a holy God.

A Financial Cost

This cost is probably the main one that keeps people from growing up spiritually. You see, before we were Christians, we thought our stuff was our stuff. But once we were adopted into the family of God and began to grow in our relationship with God, we realized our stuff was not our stuff. Our stuff is God's stuff. God wants some of His stuff given as a worship sign to Him. On every deal made, every bonus, every little bit of compensation, we are to give to God.

Spiritual adolescents rarely count the cost of what it

means to grow up spiritually. They don't want to pay the relational, time, or financial costs.

And what do they do instead? They take potshots at the church. They try to cut down mature believers. They say . . .

"This church is just too big. I get lost." If I had four tickets to the Cowboys' home opener and said, "These fifty-yard tickets are yours," I doubt if any person in the greater Dallas–Fort Worth area would refuse them. People don't have any problem sitting in Texas Stadium with tens of thousands of other people.

If I gave away a $10,000 gift certificate to the Galleria Mall, I don't think any person in Texas would turn down the gift because the Galleria has too many stores.

If you read and study about the church in the New Testament, you are going to discover that most of those churches had tens of thousands of members. If a church is in an area that has a lot of people, the church should have a lot of members.

"Your ministry just isn't deep enough." The truth is, if most people tried to apply only 10 percent of what they know about God's Word, they would have plenty to keep them occupied. We need to know God's Word, and we need to understand it. But beyond that, we need to act on it. The Bible was not written for our information, but for our application. Jesus said, "Do it. Apply it." If you get

involved with a church in order to do what God's Word says, you'll find that church is plenty deep enough.

"The church is full of hypocrites." True. I'm a hypocrite. I admit it right now. But do you know what a hypocrite is? A hypocrite is a person who says he will do something, and then he doesn't do it. A hypocrite acts as if he is on fire and sometimes he fails. I'm guilty of that. And so is every other person I know. Jesus said He came to heal those who need a physician, not those who think they are perfect. He came to help those of us who know we are hypocrites. A church *should* be full of sickly sinners who know they are sick and have come to try to get well.

The Upside to Maturity

There are two notable benefits to spiritual maturity.

Greater Courage

Are you aware that psychologists have identified 645 types of fear? I'll cite the top 3:

1. Fear of Death. We all have a desire to live. God gives us this desire. The fact is we all are going to die eventually. If you are outside of Christ, that is something you *should* fear. The Bible says one day we are going to face a holy and loving God, and He is going to ask us this question: "Have you received My pardon?"

Have you? It's a yes or no question. If your answer is yes, you'll spend eternity in heaven, and you have nothing to fear in death. If your answer is no, you will be eternally separated from God.

Spiritually mature people have an ability to face death courageously.

2. Fear of loneliness. I am in dialogue with many lonely people. They have no real community at work, no real community in their neighborhood. They just don't know anyone they can call a real friend. We all long for relationships. Primarily we long for a personal relationship with Jesus Christ, and secondarily we long for relationships with other human beings. If you are in Christ, your relational base must be the church. There are many ports of entry for meeting people and making friends in a church. Get involved.

Spiritually mature people are involved. They not only have lifelong friends; they have eternal friends.

3. Fear of failure. Most people are fearful to step out, take a risk, challenge the unknown. Most of us say more than once in our lives, "I can't try that. I might fall flat on my face." That is one of the reasons I love the Bible. The Bible gives example after example of men and women who have fallen flat on their faces. They have messed up, taken a risk, and stumbled. If you are in Christ, Jesus knows before you fall that you are going to fumble and stumble and fail. He knows that. And His word is, "Get back up! I am going to forgive you, change you, and work on you."

If you are outside of Christ, taking a risk can be scary. But if you are in Christ, well, the Bible declares, "If God is for us, who can be against us?" (Rom. 8:31). It says, "Since we have such hope, we use great boldness of speech" (2 Cor. 3:12). It says that God is capable of working all things to our good, even our failures (Rom. 8:28).

Are you aware that the Bible says 365 times, "Fear not"? That's one "fear not" for every day of the year. It's as if God wanted that point to be obvious.

Spiritually mature people are willing to take risks. And those risks invariably lead to the expansion of the kingdom of God.

Are you allowing these fears to hold you back? Are you allowing them to keep you from growing up spiritually?

Adolescents may act brave, but theirs is a false bravado. The mature person faces life with true courage.

Greater Hope

Several years ago Lisa and I went on a mission trip to Korea. When we returned home two weeks later, we were walking up to our front door when suddenly the door flew open and LeeBeth, our three-year-old daughter, ran out. She jumped into our arms, kissed us, and said she was glad we were home. Then she said, "Put me down! Put me down!"

We did, and she immediately began to take off all her clothes.

We were startled and asked what she was doing, taking off all her clothes outside for all the neighbors to see. She said, "Where is my new outfit?"

We unbuckled our suitcases, took out the Korean outfit we had bought for her, and gave it to her. She put it on immediately.

That's hope. Lisa had told LeeBeth in a phone call that we had a new outfit for her, and LeeBeth was *expecting* that outfit to arrive when we did. She was waiting for it! Her hope was in high gear.

What are you hoping for today?

You have many reasons to be hopeful. The Bible says you have been pardoned: "There is therefore now no condemnation to those who are in Christ Jesus" (Rom. 8:1). There's no failure, no mistake, no sin that can cause God to change His mind and "unforgive" us.

All of us mess up. Abraham lied about Sarah being his wife. Moses struck a rock in anger. David committed adultery with Bathsheba. Simon Peter did the Zorro thing and cut off the ear of one of the guys who arrested Jesus. Each suffered some consequences from his sin, but he didn't experience condemnation. Condemnation means irreversible eternal punishment. Condemnation means an irreversible sentence that can never be pardoned. Condemnation means that the judge is saying, "You're behind bars for the rest of your life, and then there's the electric chair and after that hell."

We may have deadly defects. But if we are in Christ, we have hope. God wants to clean up every deadly sin in us, so we can live life to its fullest. But there is no condemnation. He always holds out hope to us. He never gives up on us.

The mature Christian experiences greater and greater hope. And that means greater and greater motivation.

The mature Christian is the guy standing on tiptoe to see what God is going to do next.

A SPARKLING FUTURE

Any person who sees a diamond taken out of a mine in South Africa and then sees that diamond set into a fourteen-carat-gold ring can hardly believe it's the same stone. We're all diamonds in the rough when we first come to Christ. We have sin's mud and crud and grime all over us.

God puts us into His washer, and then His cutter, and then His polisher. He knocks away the excess and confronts us with our deadly defects, so we can make changes, and He can turn us into the diamond that He knows is there all the time.

God will use that coach, that situation, that school, that church, that boss, that spouse, that friend as part of the process.

Don't ice God out. Don't put on your headphones,

crank up the music, and try to drown out His voice. Listen to what God is saying to you. God may be telling you to apologize to someone, stop something, start something, continue something, be something. Listen, and then do it.

If you run from God and choose to do what you please, you remain a diamond in the rough. You remain in spiritual adolescence.

If you invite God to do His work, He produces in you and through you something of great value.

Spiritual maturity costs something. But it's worth everything.

CONCLUSION

What Must We Do?

I recently went fishing with a friend. We were in a two-man "bass buster," one of those tiny little boats that is part Styrofoam and part plastic. We were having a good time catching largemouth bass left and right, floating along in the middle of the lake—and suddenly the boat stopped. We could tell we were hung up on something, but we couldn't tell what.

We did what most experienced anglers do in a situation like that. We began to rock the boat back and forth. That didn't work. Then we began to paddle furiously, as if we were on an Olympic rowing team. That didn't work.

I tried cranking up the dial on the electric trolling motor to full blast. That didn't work either.

Finally I elected to dive overboard into the coffee-black waters of the lake and feel under the boat to see what was actually there. I did not encounter the fourteen water moccasins I had feared. I discovered that a giant underwater limb had poked a hole in the front of our boat. I knew immediately that we were in serious trouble.

I came up for air and called to my friend. I let him know that if we didn't get ourselves free of that limb, we weren't going anywhere. He moved to the back of the boat to give what leverage he could with his body weight, and I went back underwater to push up on the front of the boat in an attempt to lift the boat off the limb. That worked!

Fortunately the hole was more of a surface wound than a real puncture of the boat, so we enjoyed freedom, security, and a great time of fishing for a few hours longer.

What would have happened, however, if we had been content to stay in our boat, stuck in the middle of the lake, rocking back and forth, paddling furiously, and playing with the dial on the trolling motor? The day would have been a loss, marked by senseless repetition without getting to the real root of our problem.

The seven fatal distractions are like the limb of that tree. They hang us up. They create obstacles in our lives that keep us from moving forward in freedom to live the meaningful lives God wants us to live.

We have to deal with the sin in our lives if we truly want to move forward—to grow spiritually, to mature in our relationships with others, and to be more effective witnesses for Christ. Sin doesn't go away on its own. It doesn't dissipate over time. We must face our sin—our deadly defects. We need to put on our diving masks, get under the boat, and find out what is hanging us up. Then we must confess our sin to God, be forgiven of it, and truly *repent* of it—which means to turn and walk away from it.

IT'S NEVER TOO LATE TO START

In John 5, we find Jesus making His way through the streets of Jerusalem to a pool with sick people lying around it. They weren't catching rays. They had severe health problems and disabilities. As Jesus walked toward the pool, He knelt down beside a man who had been disabled thirty-eight years. Jesus asked him, "Do you really want to be healed? Do you really want to part with your problem? Do you really want Me to change your life?"

Those seem to be questions with obvious answers. But the more you think about this situation, the more profound the questions become.

Jesus knows us better than anyone else ever can. He knows our tendency as human beings to build our lives around our problems and to set up systems around our difficulties. We get accustomed to pain. We learn to live with situations. The man might very well have been so used to his illness that he no longer thought about getting well. Going down to the pool to lie there with his friends might have become a habit.

Do you really *want* to be free of the fatal distraction that is keeping you from the fullness of God's plan for your life? Or have you accommodated sin? Have you become comfortable with your habit of sin?

If we're asked directly, we probably say, "Sure I want to be free of this!" But do we really?

Consider pride. Getting rid of pride sounds "cool" on the surface. But do we really want to part with our feelings of superiority? Do we really think we can live without comparing ourselves to others and feeling smarter, stronger, or better-looking than another person?

What about anger? We may say we'd like to be free of it. But deep inside, are we afraid that we might miss the adrenaline rush that comes when we boil over in rage?

Getting rid of greed sounds wonderful until it cuts into our buying habits. Gluttony sounds like a good thing to get rid of until Sunday brunch rolls around. Freeing ourselves from lust sounds like a good idea until we realize that we are going to miss the excitement of our sexual fantasies.

We have a hard time getting rid of our trash for several reasons:

- Our trash has been accumulating for a long time. We have had sin in our lives since birth, and without a doubt since puberty. Our sin becomes like an old pair of running shoes. It doesn't serve us very well, but it feels good. We've grown accustomed to sinning.

- Our trash has become part of our identity. Many people have decided, *This is just the way I am.* In some ways, we like the fact that we are a type A personality, or we orchestrate the lives of others, or we live over the top in excess. We have bought in to the lie that it's important to like ourselves "just the way we are." We have learned to like our own sinfulness.

- Our trash has a good benefit. Over time, we have found a payoff to our particular desire to sin. We like the feelings; we like the temporary rush; we like the short-term benefits. We use our sin to excuse our failures, to manipulate other people, and to bring sympathy to ourselves. Sin works for us, and we like the benefit it brings— even if only for an hour or a day.

IT'S NEVER TOO LATE TO START OVER

Does there come a time when it's too late to start over? Never!
Several years ago I flew back to the Dallas–Fort

Worth airport after speaking in Colorado, and my family was there to greet me. I carried a black leather attaché as I got off the plane. In it were my Bible and the upcoming Sunday's sermon. While helping my wife put the twins into their car seats, I placed that leather attaché on top of the vehicle and then drove off. The attaché flipped off the top of the car and was never to be seen again—at least by me.

I was upset, angry, and frustrated. I had used that Bible ever since we started the church I pastor. The leather attaché was a gift from my parents. And besides all that, I had to rewrite my sermon notes. I vowed to my wife and family, and to myself, that I would never put anything on top of a car again as long as I lived.

I kept that promise for about four months. Then one Wednesday evening as I left the church, I again was helping Lisa put the twins in the car. And again, I put my notebook and Bible on top of the vehicle. We had brought two cars to church that evening, so I said to Lisa that I'd take our son, E. J., with me, and we'd follow her home. I talked to some friends for a couple of minutes, and then E. J. and I turned to go to my car. A sick feeling hit me. I said, "E. J., did Daddy give you a notebook and Bible to hold?" Of course I hadn't.

We hurried to my car, I threw E. J. into his seat in the back of the car, and I raced out of the parking lot and cruised down the boulevard I was sure Lisa had taken. I had my bright lights on searching for my stuff, which I was sure must be lying somewhere in the middle of the road. I had gone about four miles, at a rate of about three miles an hour, when I saw my Bible in the middle of the boulevard. I pulled over into the grass and ran across four lanes of traffic to retrieve that Bible, thanking God all the way that I hadn't lost it. It was a Bible I had owned about fourteen years and it was filled with notes. I looked all around for my notebook, which had the next Sunday's sermon in it. Then I reasoned that since the notebook was heavier, it had perhaps stayed on top of the car a bit longer, perhaps all the way home.

Sure enough, after making a couple of turns, I spied my notebook in the middle of another street. I pulled over, dodged some cars, and picked up the notebook, hoping to find my sermon. No sermon there. Then I glanced down the road, and about 150 yards away, I saw fragments of my eighteen-page sermon research billowing in the breeze. I sprinted down the road, running through cars like a football player moving through the pack, and retrieved as much as I could.

Was I making progress? I felt that I was. At least the second time I was able to retrieve, with considerable effort, what I had lost. Did I vow again never to put anything on the top of a car? Yes. I didn't let that slipup keep me from trying to change this bad habit.

So far, so good.

What happens when we find that we have erred again and have fallen into one of the seven deadly sins?

We must decide again that we are going to confess our

sin to God and make yet another commitment to live the way God has commanded us to live.

We must never allow ourselves to reach the point where we say, "I don't care anymore." No matter how many times we may fail or slip or mess up or fall off the wagon, we must get up and try again. Each time we must ask the Lord's forgiveness—and we can be assured that anytime we ask sincerely for the Lord's forgiveness, He gives it. Each time, we must ask again for the Lord's help—and just as He forgives, He remains willing to help us.

Jesus said, "I am with you always, even to the end of the age" (Matt. 28:20). He doesn't leave us even for a second. He doesn't give up on us or chalk us up as failures. We must believe in our ability to refrain from the seven fatal distractions as much as Jesus believes in *His* ability to help us refrain from them!

SEVEN HELPS FOR DEALING WITH DEFECTS

Here are seven ideas to help you deal with the deadly defects:

1. *Tackle Each Character Defect One at a Time*

Next time you watch a football game, watch the defense. The defenders don't try to tackle every person on the offense. They try to tackle the guy with the ball.

Take on the deadly defect that you believe is causing

the most damage to your life. We struggle with all of the seven fatal distractions, but we generally have a greater struggle with one of them. Name it and go after it.

2. Focus Your Prayers for Yourself

Proverbs 17:24 offers this insight: "Wisdom is in the sight of him who has understanding, but the eyes of a fool are on the ends of the earth." In other words, "The wise person aims for a goal, but a fool goes off in many directions." Focus your efforts. Focus your concern. Focus your prayers.

Begin to pray what I call laser prayers.

Don't just say, "Lord, I admit I have a problem with anger. Please remove it from my life." Instead, break down that prayer into short, specific requests: "Tomorrow, between nine and eleven o'clock, I'm going to be in a business meeting, and usually in this particular meeting I let everybody present 'have it.' God, please replace my anger with humility and love between nine and eleven o'clock tomorrow morning. Help me to make my points without raging at those present." That's a laser prayer.

Don't just pray, "God, please remove lust from my life." Instead, pray, "Heavenly Father, I have a date tonight that will probably last from eight o'clock to midnight. Please help me see this person as a whole person—a person who matters to You and not as an object to be used."

Don't just pray, "God, help me overcome my greed." Get the laser fired up. Pray, "Father, I'm going to the mall tomorrow with a friend. Please help me to admire the beautiful things I see without feeling I have to own them."

Be specific about what you desire for God to do for you.

3. Focus on Victory One Day at a Time

Jesus said we are to pray, "Give us this day our daily bread" (Matt. 6:11). He didn't say, "Please load me up for the next month." We were created to breathe sixty or seventy times a minute. Our hearts were created to beat about seventy times a minute. Our bodies were made to be fed daily, and they usually perform best if they are fed four or five times a day, a little bit each time. We were made to sleep about eight hours out of twenty-four. We were designed by God to be *daily* creatures.

Focus on your victories one day at a time. Celebrate your victories periodically. When you realize that you have gone twenty-one days without giving in to anger, lust, or gluttony, throw yourself a party! Celebrate what God and you are doing together in your life! Doing this will keep you focused on success, not failure.

4. Choose to Act Even When You Don't Feel Like It

Alcoholics Anonymous has a slogan: "Fake it until you make it." In other words, choose to act in a way that is *opposite* the deadly defect in your life, even if you don't feel like acting that way. It's easier to act your way into a feeling than to feel your way into a right action. Pray, "God, I want to be obedient to You even though it seems weird to me. I am going to obey You in this even though I don't like it very much." Once you start the process, God will allow the feelings to catch up with you.

5. Don't Rely Solely on Your Willpower

Remember that it is your *will* but His *power*. Rely on God's power more than your power. Ask for His help.

Jeremiah made this astute observation: "Can the Ethiopian change his skin or the leopard its spots? Then may you also do good who are accustomed to do evil" (Jer. 13:23). In your own strength, it's impossible to change your identity, your character, or your behavior. However, as Paul said, "I can do all things through Christ who strengthens me" (Phil. 4:13). By ourselves, we can do nothing. With Christ, we can accomplish every goal that is worth going after.

My family and I generate a great deal of trash. With four young children, the amount of trash we produce can be staggering at times. One challenge I have faced in taking out the trash is *not* the size of the trash bags or the number of them. The challenge is the six-inch gap at the bottom of the fence that separates our yard from that of our neighbors, and the two man-eating Rottweilers that live beyond that fence. One day I was shooting baskets, and I missed a shot. The ball bounced over to the other side of the fence, and I immediately heard growls and then a loud indication that the ball was deflating. The two dogs ate my Michael Jordan basketball! I share that only to let you know that they are not to be taken lightly.

One night as I was dragging three heavy-duty, extra-large trash bags toward the trash can, one of these dogs snagged the bottom of a trash bag and began to pull that bag under the fence. We had a serious tug-of-war, and I had a major mess to clean up afterward.

When you make the decision to take out the character trash of your life, you are going to find that there may be more trash than you had counted on. One level of trash sometimes gives way to another.

You are also going to discover that the evil one, Satan, the father of lies, the ultimate Rottweiler in the spirit realm, is going to attack you at every opportunity. He's going to growl at you just low enough so that you alone can hear him, and in a tone of voice that may sound more comforting than menacing, "Don't do it. You don't have to take the trash out. Everything will be okay. You have enough willpower to take care of this and not involve God."

Keep in mind what will happen if you don't take the trash out. It will stink up your life and rot away at your very soul. It will attract all kinds of vermin and disease. Steer clear of the fence that divides your life from that of the enemy. Head straight for the trash can as fast as you can!

6. *Associate with People Who Will Help You, Not Hinder You*

An amazing thing happens when you look back and think about all of the people whom the Lord has used for good in your life. I encourage you to take a few minutes and recall some who have helped you become who you are today. Who taught you? Who guided you? Who helped you? Who loved you unconditionally? Be grateful for their help.

And then choose to get into relationship with someone you trust who can help you overcome your foremost deadly character defect. God has someone in mind to help you overcome your tendency toward a particular sin. Find that person and work with him.

The Bible teaches that once we realize the root of our problem, we need to confess our problem to someone else. A person in my church once asked me, "Ed, do you mean confess it to someone with skin on?"

Yes, that's exactly what I mean. James 5:16 tells us, "Confess your trespasses to one another, and pray for one another, that you may be healed."

The Bible doesn't say to tell everybody our sins. It says to tell "one another." That means to tell somebody— another Christian, someone you trust, a person who can keep your confidence.

This very idea causes a lot of people to panic. Their minds immediately start racing: *If I tell this person, he'll never speak to me again. If I tell that person, he'll never associate with me. If I tell her, she'll never be able to look me in the eye.*

Find someone who has a mature walk with the Lord, someone you consider to be a mentor in the faith. It might be a pastor, a Christian counselor, or even a friend who lives a long-distance phone call away. Confess your sins only to a person who can keep a secret.

Don't call the local radio talk show with your sin. Don't go on a national tell-all TV program with your fault. Tell a person who will pray for you and pray with you that you might be forgiven of your sin and not repeat it.

But do tell. In confessing your sin, you are putting yourself in position for a remarkable change to take place in your heart. Confession of sin can bring about immense freedom from guilt and shame. It can set you free to love others with an open and generous heart. It can free you to share the gospel. It can free you to be your real self.

You may be thinking, *But what do I say to this person? What kind of speech should I rehearse? Do I need to use particular words?*

No speech or formula is required. Simply look the person in the eye, and say, "You know what? When I'm angry, here is what I do." Or say, "When I see something I really want but can't really afford, here's how I feel." Give examples. Tell how you treat your family, your best friend, your coworkers, and total strangers. Admit to the person who is listening to you, "I'm not sure why this is happening."

By confessing your sins to another person, you actually hear yourself describe your behavior. At times, you may realize what you are doing and why you are acting the way you are acting when you hear yourself admit for the first time that you have a problem.

7. *Pursue Progress, Not Perfection*

Life is about progress and process. None of us are ever going to arrive at perfection, but all of us are called to move closer to it.

Keep in mind always that God is with you, and He loves you no matter where you are in your life and no matter what you are struggling with.

My daughter LeeBeth is approaching her teenage years now. I loved her when she was five, I'll love her when she is fifteen, and I'll love her when she is fifty. I don't always approve of or like everything LeeBeth does or says, but my love for her is unchanging. She is my daughter, and I love her at every stage of her growth. The same is true for each of my children.

God feels the same way about you. He loves you, even as He desires more for you. He is present to forgive your past, assist your present, and believe for your future. Philippians 1:6 is an excellent verse to memorize: "He who has begun a good work in you will complete it until the day of Jesus Christ." God will never give up on you. He isn't a quitter. He is in for the long haul.

Keep that perspective about your life. You aren't who you once were. And you still aren't who you will be one day. You are a work in progress.

Jesus Christ stands ready and willing to help you overcome the seven deadly sins.

Are you ready?

Are you willing?

Make the answer "YES!"